PORTRAIT OF MANCHESTER

THE *PORTRAIT* SERIES

Portrait of Birmingham
Vivian Bird

Portrait of the Broads
J. Wentworth Day

Portrait of the Burns Country
Hugh Douglas

Portrait of Cambridge
C. R. Benstead

Portrait of the Channel Islands
Raoul Lempriere

Portrait of the Chilterns
Annan Dickson

Portrait of the Clyde
Jack House

Portrait of Cornwall
Claude Berry

Portrait of the Cotswolds
Edith Brill

Portrait of Dartmoor
Vian Smith

Portrait of Devon
D. St. Leger-Gordon

Portrait of Dorset
Ralph Wightman

Portrait of County Durham
Peter A. White

Portrait of Edinburgh
Ian Nimmo

Portrait of Exmoor
J. H. B. Peel

Portrait of Gloucestershire
T. A. Ryder

Portrait of the Highlands
W. Douglas Simpson

Portrait of the Isle of Man
E. H. Stenning

Portrait of the Isle of Wight
Lawrence Wilson

Portrait of the Isles of Scilly
Clive Mumford

Portrait of the Lakes
Norman Nicholson

Portrait of Lancashire
Jessica Lofthouse

Portrait of Liverpool
Howard Channon

Portrait of London River
Basil E. Cracknell

Portrait of Manchester
Michael Kennedy

Portrait of the New Forest
Brian Vesey-Fitzgerald

Portrait of Northumberland
Nancy Ridley

Portrait of Peakland
Crichton Porteous

Portrait of the Pennines
Roger A. Redfern

Portrait of the Quantocks
Vincent Waite

Portrait of the Severn
J. H. B. Peel

Portrait of the Scott Country
Marion Lockhead

Portrait of the Shakespeare Country
J. C. Trewin

Portrait of the Shires
Bernard Newman

Portrait of Skye and the Outer Hebrides
W. Douglas Simpson

Portrait of Snowdonia
Cledwyn Hughes

Portrait of Somerset
Bryan Little

Portrait of Surrey
Basil E. Cracknell

Portrait of the Thames
J. H. B. Peel

Portrait of the Trent
Peter Lord

Portrait of the Wye Valley
H. L. V. Fletcher

Portrait of Yorkshire
Harry J. Scott

Portrait of
MANCHESTER

MICHAEL KENNEDY

Photographs by
Sefton Samuels

ROBERT HALE · LONDON

© *Michael Kennedy 1970*
First published in Great Britain 1970

ISBN 0 7091 1812 0

Robert Hale & Company
63 Old Brompton Road
London S.W.7.

Printed and bound in Great Britain by
C. Tinling & Co. Ltd, London and Prescot

FOR ESLYN

CONTENTS

Preface 11

I Ancient and Modern 13

II Georgian Boom Town 28

III "Look Here Upon This Picture . . ." 37

IV ". . . And On This" 49

V Caps of Liberty 61

VI Princes' Palaces 77

VII What Price the Arts? 89

VIII This Sporting Life 111

IX News and Views 123

X Panorama 136

XI Greater Manchester 151

XII Strictly Personal 169

XIII What Next? 180

Index 187

ILLUSTRATIONS

Gateway House on Piccadilly Station approach *facing page* 24

The new dominates the old in this aerial view of the city centre. Among the major buildings which can be seen, looking from left to right, are the Law Courts, the Cathedral, Kendal Milne's, John Rylands Library, the Royal Exchange, the CIS, the Free Trade Hall, the Town Hall and Extension and the Central Library. In the centre foreground is St John Street (*Airviews Ltd*) *between pages* 24 & 25

Former house of the Tattons, Wythenshawe Hall *facing page* 25

Pre-1939 houses on the Wythenshawe estate   25

The Hallé's guiding spirit, Barbirolli at rehearsal   32

L. S. Lowry, artist of Lancashire   32

Georgian elegance in King Street   33

1806 oasis in Mosley Street: the Portico Library   48

St Peter's Square and the Central Library   49

The Law Courts in Crown Square   64

Modern setting for modern art in the Whitworth   65

Theatre workshop in the university   80

Humphrey Chetham in his baronial hall   81

Monastic calm for scholars in John Rylands Library   96

On the Ship Canal   97

Engineering marvel, the Barton Aqueduct   97

Looking towards the Cathedral High Altar   112

Fletcher Moss Gallery, once the Old Parsonage, Didsbury 113

ILLUSTRATIONS

Pupils on their way to Manchester Grammar School 113

The CIS building, highest in Manchester 128

Hulme before rehousing began 129

As it is today 129

The Piccadilly Plaza 144

Elisabeth Frink's "Flight" in Ringway concourse 145

Jodrell Bank, technology in a Cheshire field 145

Medieval survivor, the Old Wellington Inn 160

Albert Square in the snow 161

Guardian sanctum, C. P. Scott's office 176

Portland Street palace, Watts' warehouse 176

Barnes Wallis building, Institute of Science and Technology 177

Map of Central Manchester *page* 12

Map of Greater Manchester *pages* 14 & 15

(Special acknowledgement is made to officials of Manchester Corporation and of the John Rylands Library for their help regarding some of the illustrations.)

western section of Northern England. To the east is the Pennine Range which divides Lancashire, Westmorland and Cumberland from Yorkshire, Durham and Northumberland. Its foothills reach nearly to the site of the city. To the west, the marshland of Chat Moss and the River Mersey provided a natural defence of the southern part of Lancashire. Manchester was built at the confluence of the Medlock and the Irk with the larger River Irwell, which was easily navigable for most ships of bygone days.

It seems probable that the Ancient Britons had a settlement on the banks of the Irwell before the Romans came to Britain in 55 B.C. The Romans built a fort in the Castlefield area, near where the Rochdale Canal and Bridgewater Street are today, during the governorship of Julius Agricola (A.D. 78–86) and called it Mamucium, 'the place of a breast-like hill'. The name was corrupted into 'Mancunium', from which the present-day description of a citizen of Manchester as a Mancunian derives. Traces of the Roman occupation have been almost totally obscured by later developments, despite assiduous and continuing archaeological work. Almost every attempt to give any account of Mamucium is so bespattered with 'perhaps' and 'probably' and 'possibly' and 'presumably' that the only safe assertions to make are that the Romans were there and in the fifth century they left.

The most convincing relic of their presence is their roads. Watling Street came into Castlefield from Knutsford and continued north through Strangeways and Prestwich. Another road crossed the Irwell through Salford, another led to the east through Failsworth and Oldham towards what is now Huddersfield, another crossed Blackstone Edge into Yorkshire, and a fifth, the present London Road via Stockport, went in the direction of Buxton. A recital of these names emphasises what is still a primary feature of the modern city: situated just a few miles over the Lancashire border with Cheshire on its southern side and at the base of the Pennine slopes on its northern, it is within easy distance of some of the most beautiful and varied scenery in Britain. This geographical accident is the prime cause of another important aspect of Manchester, namely that despite its pronounced individuality—sometimes in the past, it must be said, over-assertive perhaps because of an inferiority complex—it is a cosmopolitan place, never more so than today when nineteen consuls are needed for its inhabitants.

For that reason, defining the Manchester Man is becoming increasingly difficult. From its earliest days of commercial importance Manchester has attracted Yorkshiremen, Scotsmen and North-easterners to work in it. Its colony of Germans during the nineteenth century is often mentioned, but often exaggerated in numbers: in 1901, for example, 756 men and 563 women of German origin lived there. In 1841 a tenth of the population was Irish (over 30,000 of them). Today if you walk around the city the accents you will hear are chiefly standard English, B.B.C. regional, southern suburban or foreign. Very rarely will you be lucky enough to hear the rich, truly Lancastrian dialect, the Mancunian accent, so far as one can be said to exist, being a rather slovenly, unattractive, urbanised patois. Manchester is a business city, not a residential one, and today its airport connects it with the world, the train journey from Euston to the centre of Manchester is 160 minutes—and shorter than that if you use the comfortable Pullman (and shorter still when the 200 m.p.h. trains come into service)—while the M6 passes close enough for easy access by road from North and South. By 1980 junctions to five motorway routes will be near Manchester: those to Liverpool; to Preston; over the Pennines to Leeds and, eventually, to Hull; the North Cheshire motorway from Liverpool to Ringway airport; and the M6, linked soon to the M1 in the south and being extended to Scotland. Not only does this make Manchester a strategic hub of communications for trade, it enables it to justify a claim to be a tourist centre, within very speedy reach of the Lake District, the Peak National Park, Snowdonia and Yorkshire.

If the Manchester Man is hard to define, so of course is Manchester itself. What do we mean by the elegant, comfortable-sounding name Manchester? It was always amusing to point out to strangers that Manchester's racecourse (now no more), Manchester United's ground, the Manchester Ship Canal and Manchester's docks all shared one thing in common: none was in Manchester. The City of Manchester is quite a small place, no more than 13 miles long and 5 wide. During the week about a million people work, shop or enjoy themselves in it. But its population is only 595,000, a decline from 700,000 in 1952. (By 1981 a further decline to 550,000 is expected.) The true Mancunian always speaks of this city area as 'Town'. Going into Town means a day in Manchester.

What is generally meant by Manchester, though, is the Manchester area, and here there are two choices. First you can count it as including Salford, Stretford, Sale, Altrincham, Prestwich, Cheadle, Didsbury, Stockport, Swinton, Eccles, Urmston, Partington and Bramhall—an inner ring of towns which retain individuality but can hardly escape absorption into the life of Manchester, the creeping giant at their centre. Or you can select an area which it would be folly to call Greater Manchester, since several of its constituents are of ferociously independent means and outlook, and which is therefore tactfully but clumsily known as the South-east Lancashire-North-east Cheshire Conurbation (horrible but unavoidable word). The conurbation takes in Bolton, Bury, Oldham and Rochdale, which in itself is sufficient guarantee that any attempt to 'Mancunianise' them completely, if I may coin another horrible word, is doomed to failure—or success only against bitter and long strife—by virtue of their rugged qualities of local patriotism. Nevertheless, Manchester is the pulse of the conurbation, 379 square miles of Lancashire and Cheshire with a population approaching 3 million, one of the greatest centres of industry, commerce and manufacture in the civilised world.

To trace the spread of this conurbation is to trace the social history of Manchester, and at the same time to answer the question: why the decline in the city's population? Simply because those who came into the city for business have, as their prosperity has increased and means of travel have improved, moved further and further out into Cheshire or Derbyshire. Let us go back once again to pre-medieval times. Somehow, between the departure of the Romans and the arrival of the Normans, Mamucium became Manigeceastre and Mamecestre. In 870 the Danes laid it waste; in 919 or 923 Edward the Elder, son of Alfred the Great, sent a Mercian force from Thelwall in Cheshire to repair it and to man the ruined Roman fort.

Some years later most of Lancashire was divided into six 'hundreds', each with a capital manor, from which the hundred took its name, and some subsidiary manors. Salford was a hundred and Manchester its inferior manor. There lies the source of some much later local rivalry! Yet Salford had no church until the seventeenth century (1635) and was under the ecclesiastical jurisdiction of Manchester. The first church in Manchester was

St. Mary's, which stood on or near the site of the present cathedral overlooking the Irwell, an area still known as St. Mary's Gate. In 1028 King Canute is supposed to have taken an interest in Manchester, Knott Mill traditionally being said to derive its name from Canute's Mill, the revenue from which he is said to have appropriated to alleviate taxation. But historians think it was another Canute and that John Knott, of Knott Mylne, who died in 1597, was the originator of Knott Mill.

Manchester's history for the 500 years after the Norman Conquest is hardly the stuff of which romance is made. Manchester was, after all, only a village. Most of what is now Lancashire was given by William I to a Norman Knight, Roger of Poitou, and it was an area of forest and marshland. Probably the population of the Salford Hundred at the time of Domesday Book, 1086, was about 3,000, some say even fewer. The hundred had one priest, and a piece of ploughland stretching from Deansgate to the Irwell was set aside, free of all tax except Danegeld, for the churches of St. Michael and St. Mary. (In the summer, city workers today sun themselves in a part of this field, known as 'The Parsonage', near Kendal Milne's department store.) It is typical of the vagueness of all Manchester's early history that no one certainly knows if these churches really were in Manchester, or at Radcliffe, or (doubtfully) at Ashton-under-Lyne.

Sir Roger was banished by King Henry I in 1102. Henry started the process of increasing the estates of some of the less important knightly families, thereby laying the foundation of a stronger, loyal baronage. One of the new baronies was that of Manchester, which was given to Albert Grelley or his son Robert. This family already held land in the Blackburn Hundred and had estates in Lincolnshire and Suffolk. Salford was not included in the new barony, and the capital manor eventually became a royal possession as part of the Duchy of Lancaster. Queen Elizabeth II is Lady of the Royal Manor of Salford.

Which member of the Grelley family first went to live in Manchester is, again, uncertain, but it seems to have been Robert, the fifth baron. He built his manor house near the church on what is now the site of Chetham's Hospital School, this area being the oldest part ot the city, the hub from which it has spoked out to become the conurbation of today. Here he was near the Irk, whose powerful waters provided power for corn-grinding. To build his home he needed timber and stone. The former he fetched from the forest at Bradford. In those days a dene, or valley, 40 yards wide and nearly 40 feet deep, ran along the north side of what is now Hanging Ditch and Cateaton Street. Grelley built a wooden bridge over the dene or hollow (hangan) ditch so that the timber could be brought across. (Deansgate, incidentally, derives its name from this valley and means literally the valley-way.) He also built another bridge over the Irk at the end of Hunt's Bank so that stone could be brought from the quarries at Collyhurst. Robert was one of the barons present at Runnymede when King John signed Magna Carta in 1215. For this he was excommunicated by the Pope; and eight months after Runny-mede, when John had reneged on his promises, he was stripped of his lands by the King, who died before his edict could take final effect.

Robert lived for another fourteen years. In 1222 he was granted the right to hold a yearly fair, a sign that the manor was increasing in importance. This fair was held just after harvest time on Acresfield, which is now St. Ann's Square. The villagers approached the field along Toll Lane, a narrow path from Deansgate. The Lord of the Manor's officials collected tolls there on everything brought to be sold. This lane survived until 1832, when it was widened and re-named St. Ann Street. Already by the first half of the thirteenth century some sub-manors had been formed from the original manor of Manchester. Their names were Ashton-under-Lyne, Heaton Norris, Withington, Blackley, Gorton, Crumpsall, Ardwick, Openshaw, Clayton, and Didsbury —all hamlets in the fields outside the village of Manchester.

Manchester received its first charter in 1301 when Thomas Grelley came of age. (Salford had had a charter since 1230). This was to govern the town for the next 500 years. A survey made in 1282, which has survived, gives some idea of Manchester just before its charter. It had a market and it had two water-driven mills, one for corn-grinding on the Irk, the other a fulling-mill, also on the Irk. Fulling meant cleansing and thickening woollen cloth with fuller's earth, so we know that some of the villagers were weavers. There was also a common oven, in Long Millgate, and everyone had to use it for baking bread and had to pay a fee to the lord of the manor.

Weavers! Here for the first time is the word that links the

Manchester we know to that remote, scarcely imaginable country village. If you stand near the traffic lights at the bottom of Deansgate, while the cars move swiftly past the now closed Exchange station up the A56 to Bury, try for a minute to forget the twentieth century and look across to 't'owd church', the cathedral, and go back in fancy over 500 years to Manchester in the fifteenth century. The Irwell was then a wide, slow-flowing river well stocked with fish. Where Victoria Bridge crosses it today there was even then a stone bridge built in about 1368, with a small chapel on one of the piers. The cathedral, then the parish church, was there, its square tower commanding a view of fields and trees. Adjoining it was what had been the Manor House but became the College of Clergy in 1422 and is now Chetham's School. A sloping bank led to the Irk, renowned for centuries for its eels, as a writer in the seventeenth century was to remark:

> None that I ever met with were to be compared for goodness (although not large) and deliciousness of taste, to the eels caught in the Irk; unanimously ascribed to the numerousness of fulling mills that stand on that river, and say that the fat, oil and grease scoured out of the cloth make the eels palatable and fat above other river eels.

A few houses dotted here and there, and that was Manchester. All behind you were lanes, meadows, woods, swampy land and in the distance the outline of the Derbyshire hills. It doesn't seem possible. But the hills are there still, in order stood, and, as I said, you still don't have to go very far into Cheshire before you can see the deer in Dunham Park, or sail a dinghy on Pickmere, or watch rare birds at Rostherne, or play village cricket at Ashley, or walk in Lyme Park and forget that a great commercial and industrial monster is gulping and heaving and stirring only a few minutes' drive away.

If today you want all your worst illusions about Manchester confirmed approach it from the north-east, from Oldham. For the next 7 miles there stretches a continuous and depressing procession of old houses, factories, chimneys, garages. Watch your speed, because it is indeed a built-up area, built-up haphazardly, sprawling formlessly in a manner that condemns the price paid for material prosperity and its sudden opposite. But peer more closely at the houses: how well they are kept, how clean the steps, how valiant every attempt to brighten with paint the drabness of the builder's design.

From these homes, soon to be bulldozed away as they have been in Hulme and Ancoats, came the real Manchester men and women, cheerful people usually, less dour than Yorkshire folk, but still phlegmatic, unemotional on the surface, feeling deeply below it, level-headed, fair, accustomed to bad times as much as to good, loyal but not sycophantic, good friends and good haters, stubborn to a fault, generous often beyond their means. Long-suffering, too, and slow to anger, but tenacious in the fight when they felt right to be on their side. These were the people who went to hear Henry Hunt speak on St. Peter's Field in 1819; who flocked to join their county regiment in two world wars; who stood on the street corners, idle and degraded, in the Depression, when not only love but all Lancashire was on the dole. Indomitable people, most of them enjoying prosperity today, a prosperity earned by the sweat of their forefathers' brows and by more than that, for it was in Manchester that many trade unions were formed, when workers banded together in a spirit that owed not a little to the Methodist and other denominational faiths that taught them the meaning of man's dignity.

But if you approach from the south, the introduction is softer and more beguiling. Before the motorway was built you would have driven through Knutsford, Mrs. Gaskell's 'Cranford'. Then you come through leafy and prosperous Bowdon and the market town of Altrincham, to Sale and Stretford, dormitory and middle-class. Over to your left, but out of sight, is the 1,200-acre industrial estate, 200 factories, warehouses and depots known euphemistically as Trafford Park, where 80,000 workers make everything from giant transformers to cornflakes. As you leave Stretford you have a choice of two roads. Take one, and there on your left are the four floodlight-bearing pylons of United's famous ground; take the other and on your right is the even more famous Old Trafford cricket ground, the two great sports arenas separated by a Lancashire County police headquarters as if permanent arbitration was required between devotees of the summer and winter games.

As you drive on past terrace houses which have long since become the offices of small firms or agencies, past the Northumberland Hotel—where the licensee was once the bowler Cecil

Parkin, who placarded the outside of the pub with the ghastly punning slogan "Cecil Park-in Here", bless him—you come to Hulme, once a blot on the city's name but now totally cleared of its horrible, if friendly, squalor. In its place are blocks of flats, impersonal, antiseptic but necessary. And now over the Mancunian Way flyover, under the railway bridge at Knott Mill, and into Deansgate, the long thoroughfare which forms the base line of Manchester. Turn right up its many tributaries and you come to the rest of the city. Turn left and you are soon in Salford.

Deansgate alters character along its mile-length. Its start is sombre, the suburbs not yet shaken off, the frowning buildings on either side housing car salesrooms or cycling accessories or office equipment. It looks substantial and solid but strangely impermanent, as though at any moment the leases will be up, the developers will move in and all will be changed. But it's been like that for as long as most of us can remember. Then a surprise. A wide opening on the left and there, in St. John Street, is the most elegant street in Manchester, wide and short, its Georgian houses spick and span. But few people seem to notice the beauty of 'John Street' because the houses are nearly all occupied by doctors: visitors in the daytime are usually too preoccupied with their ailments to notice the architecture, visitors at night are trying, usually vainly, to find a parking space for their car before they go into the Opera House in the next street on the left, Quay Street. Once past the Quay Street lights and Deansgate becomes livelier, though architecturally more confused and incoherent. Shops' bright windows catch the eye, the anonymous architecture of the *Daily Mail* building clashes curiously with Basil Champneys' John Rylands Library, the city's last-erected Victorian Gothic masterpiece. Hereabouts are halls which perpetually seem to be advertising meetings on such subjects as "Is God Dead?", "Who are the Martians in our Midst?" and "Justice for the Manchester Martyrs". The top end of Deansgate is the most fashionable, with Kendal Milne's store on either side of the road. A little further on and we are back to our vantage-point gazing at the Cathedral, for all the world like an East Anglian wool church dumped down in a city.

If we go up those Deansgate tributaries on its eastern side we realise how sectionalised Manchester is. It would be hard to say which is the city centre: it has several centres, shopping, business

Gateway House on Piccadilly Station approach

(Overleaf) *Aerial view of the city centre*

and cultural. The longest street to right-angle off Deansgate is Market Street, like Deansgate a gradual slope, a shopping street, thronged and garish, bustling and bizarre, emerging into the large Piccadilly area, a spacious square which could be the most impressive site in the city. Ringed until the night blitz of December 1940 with warehouses, its central area has never been adequately filled during this century. A vast new cathedral, designed in the late nineteenth century by R. H. Carpenter, was one abandoned suggestion; Sir Thomas Beecham offered to build an opera house there in 1917 and then went bankrupt. The Henry Watson Music Library once had temporary and inadequate accommodation there. Manchester Royal Infirmary stood there from 1756 until 1908. Now there are sunken gardens—a delightful oasis, true enough—a bus station, and the Piccadilly Plaza 'complex', to give it the jargon name it deserves and earns, a monument to the worst in commercial development of the 1960s.

There are three other main outlets from Piccadilly—straight on from Market Street to Piccadilly Station, as some unimaginative person has re-named the much more appropriate London Road; Portland Street, the city's Rialto; and Mosley Street, described by John Dalton in 1806 as "the most elegant and retired street in the town", but a bit passé now, although the Portico Library (of which more later) still lends the northern end distinction, and Barry's art gallery gives imposing dignity to the intersection with Princess Street, another of the streams of commerce. A few more yards and we are in St. Peter's Square. The church that stood here was demolished in the first decade of this century. Now the cenotaph (by Lutyens, 1924) commemorates the dead of two wars. On one side of the square is the Central Library, built in the 1930s in a style that matched the imitation-classicism of so many of Manchester's other buildings. On another stands the Midland Hotel, unquestionably the ugliest building of any pretensions in the city but the centre of social life nevertheless, and a reminder that it was the railways above all else which gave Manchester its importance in the development of commerce in the 1830s. That Manchester's most famous hotel should be a railway hotel is only just and proper. It occupies the site once filled by the Gentlemen's Concert Hall, where Chopin played and where Charles Hallé first played in the city he was to make his home for nearly fifty years; and before that, in the 1770s,

Former house of the Tattons, Wythenshawe Hall

Pre-1939 houses on the Wythenshawe estate

by Cooper's Cottage, its garden full of flowers and fruit.

Walk or drive past the Midland and into Peter Street and history is under your feet. Here is the Free Trade Hall, and here was St. Peter's Field, the field of Peterloo. Here is Mount Street, where the magistrates assembled on that August day in 1819, in Mr. Buxton's house. Here was the Comedy Theatre, where Puccini's *La Bohème* was sung for the first time in Britain in 1897. Later the Comedy became the Gaiety Theatre, where Miss Horniman gave the city the finest theatre it has known. Here, at the back of the Free Trade Hall, is Windmill Street, and 200 years ago there was a windmill there. We are back in Deansgate, and there are two other main tributaries which lead into squares very different in character but complementary to each other.

Walk up Brazennose Street and there ahead of you, now cleaned of its eighty years' accumulation of soot and grime, is the Town Hall, that massive symbol of Manchester's self-confidence and civic pride, the greatest of all Victorian buildings, its tower like a cathedral tower of Mammon. It fills one side of Albert Square, and it is an edifice—one might almost say a temple— with its own elaborate and inimitable grandeur, spectacularly beautiful under floodlights, authoritatively municipal in sun, shadow or rain. The rest of Albert Square is undistinguished, which is right, for this splendour could brook no rival, not even the Prince Consort's admiring gaze nor Mr. Gladstone's petrified oratorical gesture as, on his pedestal, he points the way to the Midland Hotel or, as cynics used to say, to Central Station.

The other square to which St. Ann Street leads from Deansgate is St. Ann's. The church was built in 1709, reputedly by Wren but there is no authority for this belief. In Queen Anne's reign the city's fashionable houses were built here, and even today, when all is shops and showrooms and taxis, the square retains an air of gracious living. Between the church and the modern shops a paved walk leads through a short arcade into Manchester's other fashionable shopping centre, King Street, in which is the finest Georgian building in the city. At the top of King Street, before its continuation up the hill, where it completely changes character and becomes sombre and dignified as befits the street of the Bank of England and the Reform Club, it intersects with Cross Street on its way from Albert Square to its crossing with Market Street. There, on the left, is the enormous black mass of the Royal

Exchange, once the centre of the cotton industry, and on the right the old *Manchester Guardian* building, recently vacated. Through the lights Cross Street changes into Corporation Street, and now we are back in the 'Old Town', with Hanging Ditch, the Cathedral, the huddle of streets smelling deliciously of coffee and cheese, and, dominating the modern skyline, the 400-foot-high Co-operative Insurance Society building.

In later chapters a more detailed examination will be made of the men, buildings, machines and ideas which have given international fame to a city very far from devoid of historical interest to stir the romantic imagination. Here it was where Prince Charles Edward came in 1745; where John Byrom wrote "Christians Awake"; where Dalton conceived the atomic theory and Rutherford split the atom; where the singer Malibran died; where Engels studied the working conditions of the poor and sent his findings to Marx; where Hallé settled after a glittering career in the Paris salons because the town's music-lovers asked him to 'take it in hand'; where John Bright spoke against the Corn Laws; where the T.U.C. first met; where C. P. Scott came at the age of 25 to edit his cousin's failing newspaper; where David Lloyd George was born and the first Rolls-Royce car was made; where Kathleen Ferrier sang "Land of Hope and Glory" at the opening of the reconstructed Free Trade Hall; where the crowds stood silent in the February night while the footballers' coffins were brought home from Munich. Not a city of pageantry, nor of royal occasions, but a city where men of ideas have been content to work in surroundings that none call beautiful but which nonetheless command an affectionate and compelling loyalty not to be understood by the uninitiated.

How it became this city, suddenly and swiftly, is material for the next two chapters.

TWO

GEORGIAN BOOM TOWN

WHEN Thomas Grelley died in 1313 the manor of Manchester passed to the La Warr family through Thomas's sister Joan, who had married Sir John La Warr. Grelley had in fact made a formal grant of the manor to them four years earlier. Of the La Warr family the most significant was another Thomas, a priest who inherited in 1298, having been given the Manchester benefice sixteen years earlier by his brother John. Manchester's rectors hitherto had been absentees, usually having a living elsewhere. But Thomas took his duties seriously and he noted how, during his rectorship, the town grew in size. Trade had increased and many artisans had become rich, qualifying to be yeomen. Sensing a trend towards improvement and learning, La Warr applied in 1421 for a royal licence to found a College of Clergy (a warden and eight fellows) in Manchester. So the church became a collegiate church, and in 1422 John Huntington, Rector of Ashton-under-Lyne, became first Warden of Manchester, an office he was to hold for thirty-six years. He put in hand various alterations to the church, building the choir with the aisles on both sides 30 yards long and 20 yards wide, and spent £3,000 on renovating the baronial hall as a home for the clergy.

The chief characteristic of the Cathedral to this day is its remarkable width. This is principally the work of the third Warden, Ralph Langley, who took office in 1465 and immediately caused to be taken down the nave and aisles of the Early English church and rebuilt them to harmonise stylistically with Huntington's choir. He used the materials of the Early English nave. F. S. Crowther in his *The Cathedral Church of Manchester* says that "Langley's pier arches were of the greatest beauty . . .

and it would be difficult to find any examples of columns and arches in the kingdom, or elsewhere, of purer section or finer proportions than these lovely creations of Langley's genius.' The main roof beams ended in fourteen angels, each playing a different musical instrument.

Thomas La Warr was the last of his line, and by another connection on the distaff side the barony passed to the West family in 1427. The Wests spent little time in Manchester, being much concerned with the Wars of the Roses. Thomas West, the 15th baron, was a favourite of Henry VII, who once visited Manchester while on a visit to his mother, the Countess of Richmond, second wife of the Earl of Derby, scion of the great Lancashire family of Stanley. The Earl's son James, by his first marriage (to the sister of Warwick the King-maker), was in fact Warden of Manchester and had been since 1481. In 1509 he became Bishop of Ely, through royal influence it was said, and he is described in a Life of Erasmus as "illiterate". Be that as it may, it was he who brought over from France some skilled wood carvers, lodged them in Long Millgate, and set them to work to make the glorious carved choir stalls on the south side, those on the north side being carved by Richard Bexwicke. Stanley added chantry chapels to the church, built the chapter house and remodelled the clerestory. The carved stalls, incidentally, have unusual features: a husband in flight from his wife after dropping his jug of ale; backgammon players; rabbits roasting a huntsman; monkeys stealing from a peddler's sack, and a sow piping to her litter.

When Stanley died in 1525 he was buried on the north side of the Derby Chapel but not within the wall of the church because he died an excommunicate. Thomas Fuller, in his *Worthies of England*, gives the reason: "He blamed not the prelate for passing the summer with his brother, the Earl of Derby, in Lancashire, but for living all the winter at Somersham with one who was not his sister and who wanted nothing to make her his wife save marriage."

However he conducted his private life, Stanley helped in the establishment of the first school in Manchester in one of the chantry chapels built by Bexwicke. This was the forerunner of the free grammar school, now Manchester Grammar School, which was founded in 1515 by Hugh Oldham, Bishop of Exeter, who had been born at Crumpsall. The school buildings were next to the College of Clergy, and the school derived its income from the leases of the corn and fulling mills on the Irk. When Oldham died in 1519 he endowed the school with an income of about £29 a year, a token, as is said in the school statutes, of "the good mind which he did bear to the County of Lancaster, where the children had pregnant wit, but had been mostly brought up rudely or idly, and not in virtue, cunning, education, literature, and in good manners".

This foundation is a sure clue to the growth of prosperity in Manchester. The textile trade in South Lancashire was growing and flourishing. Woollen cloths from fleeces produced on the Pennines had for some time been made in towns to the north, Manchester being a centre for the process of 'finishing'. Coarse linens and sacks were also woven from flax grown locally. The spinning and weaving were done in the homes of cottagers and smallholders. In 1542 the privilege of sanctuary was transferred from Manchester to Chester because those seeking sanctuary sometimes stole yarn or broke into the mills. From the Act which made this change we have an early description stating that Manchester "is, and hath of long time been, a town well inhabited, and the King's subjects inhabitants of the town well set awork in making cloths as well of linen as of woollen". Thereby they had gained great wealth, employed much labour and attracted many strangers 'as well of Ireland as of other places within the realm' who had deposited raw materials there and opened credit accounts. The Act describes the finishing process and refers to the materials as 'cottons', though they were all linen or wool.

The first literary description of Manchester, written four years earlier by John Leland in his *Itinerary*, confirms the town's importance. He approached from the south through what is now Sale:

> I rode over Mersey water by a great bridge of timber called Crosford Bridge. . . . I passed over Corne Brooke, and after that I touched within a good mile of Manchester by Mr. Trafford's park and place. . . . Manchester on the south side of the Irwell standeth in Salfordshire, and is the fairest, best builded, quickest, and most populace town of all Lancashire. . . . There be divers stone bridges in the town, but the best of three arches is over Irwell. This bridge

divideth Manchester from Salford, the which is a large suburb to Manchester. On this bridge is a pretty little chapel.

Leland might have mentioned, but did not, that thanks to a benefactress, a member of the Bexwicke family, Manchester already possessed a public water supply at a conduit in Market Place. This conduit was an ornamental wooden building which survived until 1729. The water came from a spring at the top of what is now King Street: a reminder of its existence survives in the area today in the names Spring Gardens and Fountain Street.

During the reign of Edward VI, when religious controversy began and the Collegiate Church was disestablished and reduced to a vicarage, an Act was passed which provided that "all and every cotton called Manchester, Lancashire and Cheshire cottons" should be a certain length, width and weight. Eight years after Queen Elizabeth I came to the throne in 1558 an official measurer (ell-bearer) of cloth was appointed and ordered to live in Manchester. He had to mark and measure every length of cloth. His deputies worked in Rochdale, Bolton, Bury and Blackburn. Probably this was necessitated by exports to France, Spain and Portugal. Dealers worked in all the towns mentioned and already Manchester manufacturers had agents in London: in the cloth market at Blackwell Hall there was a 'Manchester hall' specially for Lancashire goods. One Manchester man, Anthony Mosley, worked in partnership with his brother Nicholas in London, the latter acting as exporter. Eventually Nicholas, who became Lord Mayor of London and a baronet, bought the lordship of Manchester, thus beginning the long association of this family name with the city, still commemorated in Mosley Street.

Early in the seventeenth century woollen weaving declined in Manchester. In its place came the manufacture of fustians and smallwares, both having a warp of linen yarn. Most of the small towns of Southern Lancashire engaged in the making of fustians, which became a profitable export trade. Raw cotton for draperies was imported from the Levant. As John Loudun said in his *Manchester Memoirs:*

Manchester was steadily, tenaciously and surely identifying itself with the first principles of success by unstinted application, concentration of effort, and unchallenged reputation for excellence in products, and when we realise that the machinery by which such results were obtained was of the most elementary order, crude in construction, tedious in operation, and the workshop the home of the manufacturer, we obtain the mental adjustment which places in true perspective the conditions of the period and the character of [the] people.

These people were described in 1650 as "in general the most industrious in their callings of any in the northern parts of this kingdom. . . . Want and Waste are strangers to them, ruin and disorders are foreigners from them; courtesy and charity are inhabitants with them; civility and religion dwell among them." Their descendants were to need all that courtesy and charity when want and waste and ruin ceased to be strangers and became their *doppelgänger*.

Thanks to a printed plan we know exactly how Manchester and Salford looked in 1650. Manchester was still chiefly built round the Collegiate Church and from this centre three main streets stretched into the fields. One, Long Millgate, went north along the bank of the Irk past the mills; the second, Deansgate, went south about as far as today's Peter Street junction; the third, Market Stead Lane (now Market Street), went eastwards, with shops and houses on either side backed by fields and at the end (after about a quarter of a mile) stood Mr. Lever's House, roughly where Barratt's shoe shop is today. Piccadilly was originally called Lever's Row.

There were two market places, and between them stood the Session House, where the Court Leet (government of the town) met. On its north side were the market cross, the pillory and the stocks, and on the south the conduit. There was still only the one bridge over the Irwell to Salford, but four over the Irk at Hunt's Bank, Toad Lane (Mill Brow), Milners Lane (Miller Street), and the fourth where Scotland Bridge is today. Other streets which existed then were Smithy Bank, Cateaton Street, Shudehill, Withy Grove, Hanging Ditch and Fennel Street.

Of the houses which stood then, one is still in existence today, now known as the Old Wellington Inn. It was there, in 1692, that John Byrom, author of "Christians Awake", was born five months before his father, a linen draper, bought Kersal Cell at Salford. His uncle, Joseph Byrom, is an interesting example of one of the first really wealthy traders in Manchester, as W. H. Thomson has shown in his invaluable *History of Manchester to 1852*. He amassed

The Hallé's guiding spirit, Barbirolli at rehearsal

L. S. Lowry, artist of Lancashire

cash and property within 50 years on an astonishing scale. By 1709 he was worth £10,000 and half as much again a few years later, despite the amount he spent on land deals. It is no wonder the *Thesaurus Geographiae* of 1694 described Manchester as "the most populous and thriving town of this country. . . . The inhabitants have grown proportionately to their incredible growth in trade. . . . They have more public buildings than are commonly to be met with in other country towns." One of these was a Nonconformist chapel later known as Cross Street Chapel, opened on 24th June 1694. A woman visitor to Manchester, Celia Fiennes, wrote in 1697 of the town's "very substantial buildings . . . not very lofty but mostly of brick and stone. . . . The market place is large; it takes up two street lengths where the market is kept for their linen cloth cotton tickings which is the manufacture of the town."

Another thirty years were to see even further change. Daniel Defoe in *Defoe's Tour* (1727) writes of the further increase of business, buildings and people in the town:

> abundance not of new houses only, but of new streets of houses are added, as also a new church, dedicated to St. Ann, and they talk of another and a fine new square, so that the town is almost double to what it was some years ago. . . . Manchester, for the industry of its inhabitants, is often compared by travellers to the most industrious towns of Holland; the smallest children being all employed and earning their bread.

In 1721 the chief traders—Lees of Oldham, Byrom and Lightbowne—had sponsored an Act of Parliament to make the Irwell and Mersey navigable up to Hunt's Bank, by building locks, thus linking Manchester with Liverpool and the sea. Roads, too, were improved and turnpiked.

The wealthy manufacturers were the builders of the new houses, fine Georgian houses which were, alas, all swept away years ago. Joseph Marriott, for instance, a threadmaker who was the first to install (in 1721) an engine for the stamping and dressing of thread needing only one man to operate it, built a mansion in Brown Street. Mr. Marsden's in Market Stead Lane was another. Marriott's Court and Marsden Square commemorate them today. Edward Byrom built a fine house in Quay Street (Kay Street, then) not far from the quay he allowed to be constructed on his land

Georgian elegance in King Street

fronting the Irwell. In King Street, St. Ann's Square and Deansgate imposing houses went up.

In 1729 the lord of the manor, Sir Oswald Mosley, built Manchester's first Exchange, a two-storey colonnaded edifice which stood where Marks and Spencer's store is today. The ground floor was open and was used as a market. In the large upper room the Court Leet sat and theatrical performances were given. (Manchester's first theatre was built in Marsden Street in 1753.) Horse-racing began at Kersal in June 1729, not without strong religious opposition especially from John Byrom. All this presumes prosperity. But there were other signs. A plan to build a new workhouse was rejected in 1729. In 1752, when the population of Manchester and Salford was about 18,000 in 2,800 houses, the town's first infirmary (twelve beds) was opened in Garden Street, Withy Grove. Within four years this had proved too small, and a new hospital, costing over £2,000, was built in what is now Piccadilly, where it was removed from the bustle of the town and could easily be extended. It had eighty beds and was surrounded by trees, walks and flower beds. A contemporary writer who described Manchester then as "the very image of a radiant little garden city" ominously added: "a strong gust sufficed to blow the town clear of the mingling wreath of smoke that curled up from its modest chimneys". Incidentally, it should be noted that none of these early writers mentioned excessive rainfall.

The days of the 'garden city' were numbered. In 1754 direct communication with London came by coach, which covered the distance in four and a half days for a fare of two guineas; and within the next quarter of a century momentous events occurred which transformed Manchester. First was the construction by Brindley, between 1759 and 1761, of the third Duke of Bridgewater's canal, which enabled coal to be brought from the Duke's pits at Worsley into the centre of Manchester at Castlefield and cut the price of coal from 7d to 3½d per hundredweight. The most daring innovation in construction of this waterway was the stone-built Barton aqueduct, a sight which drew visitors from miles around. Its 1894 successor became the cause of massive traffic delays until the M62 road over the Ship Canal eased the situation. Eventually the canal was extended to Runcorn, Cheshire, enabling food supplies from a wider area to reach Manchester. Bad road conditions in the winter often caused severe dislocation in supplies of vegetables, potatoes and fruit from the outlying districts such as Warrington to Manchester, and led in 1757 to a famine period resulting in riots in the Shudehill district, where poverty and squalor were already developing. The extension of the canal also linked Manchester to the Midlands by way of the Grand Trunk Canal, thereby providing a cheap means of importing raw cotton into the town from Liverpool.

The second major event was the invention in 1763 of the spinning jenny, the first of a series of labour-saving pieces of machinery. It was the brain-child of a reed maker at Leigh, Thomas Highs, who named it after his daughter Jane. It was improved in 1767 by James Hargreaves. Two years later the water-frame came from Richard Arkwright; in 1779 Samuel Crompton developed the 'mule'; and the first power-loom was introduced in 1785 by Cartwright. Not only did these inventions change the cotton trade, they created a new industry: manufacture of textile machinery. Socially their biggest impact was the development of the factory, instead of the home, as the place of work. Arkwright built the first cotton spinning factory in Manchester shortly after 1780, at Shudehill. Others soon followed. Manchester became a 'boom town'. People flocked there to work from Scotland and Ireland. Foreign merchants came to set up business in the town (a Dutch firm in Spring Gardens was the first, in 1781, followed the next year by a French; the first German business house, C. F. Brandt, was established in 1783 in what is now Princess Street). Statistics tell the story dramatically.

The population was 18,000 (including Salford) in 1752; by 1758 Manchester alone had 17,000 inhabitants, and fifteen years later 24,386; another fourteen years and the population was 43,000 and in 1801, the year of the first official census, 70,409. Over the same period the value of exports of cotton goods rose from £46,000 in 1751 to £200,000 in 1764 and to nearly £5½ million by 1800. Manchester had become the loom of the world.

Almost everything that gave Manchester its character, its place in history, its buildings, its politics, its culture occurred between 1780 and the accession of Queen Victoria in 1837. Thomas Maurice, writing his memoirs some years later, spoke of Manchester in 1775 as "rather in a progressive state to grandeur than the magnificent place it has since become. It could boast even then, however, a noble square or two, and many elegant and spacious streets, while new squares and new streets of still greater extent and elegance were everywhere rising around." It achieved its wealth despite one custom which apparently was a never-ending source of surprise to visitors from the South—the custom of having dinner (or lunch, to be accurate) from 1 p.m. to 2 p.m. A writer in *Blackwood's Magazine* in the late 1830s eloquently recorded his amazement:

> Rich, poor, ignorant, learned, Destructive, Conservative, Dissenter, Churchman—the mass—yes, the mass, all dine at One!! This would be a deplorable state of things for any people; but, for Manchester warehousemen, with their clerks, porters, servants, friends, visitors, all to rush at ONE o'clock to dinner, leaving the bank, the manufactory, the office—all—all—to take care of themselves—is that which no man in his senses would be justified in believing, unless ocular demonstration prevented him from doubting the accuracy of the fact. In a vast many houses of business, not even one solitary clerk is to be found at the counting-office from one to two—and, not in one out of fifty is the principal to be seen from one to three! Thus, the very heart of the day, the very best portion for mercantile operations—when the light is best, when the head is clearest, and when, in almost all countries professing to be civilised, men devote their time to their most important avocations, is consumed at Manchester by the DINNER!

Perhaps this was the origin of "What Manchester thinks today. . . ."

THREE

"LOOK HERE UPON THIS PICTURE..."

MANCHESTER in 1780, although acknowledged as one of the country's leading towns, was still officially a market town, governed feudally and unrepresented in the House of Commons. Nobody minded much about this, and as usual there was a good practical reason. A free market for labour was available, and the cause of a large middle-class. Everyone with some ingenuity, with an idea to sell, was welcome in Manchester trade, whereas, as a contemporary author put it, other towns had corporations who made regulations "to favour freemen in exclusion of strangers; and indeed nothing could be more fatal to its trading interest, if it should be incorporated and have representatives in Parliament".

Two strata were clearly identifiable in the town's social and cultural life: a small group of intellectuals and upper middle-class merchants and a much larger *nouveau riche*, local men who had started with no education and no money but plenty of ingenuity and industry and had made their fortunes. Some of this latter class retained a fellow-feeling with their workers, from whose ranks they had risen, others frankly despised and ill-treated them. Samuel Curwen, an American visitor to Manchester in 1777, was unimpressed by its people:

> The disposition and manners of this people ... are inhospitable and boorish.... In all the manufacturing towns there is a jealousy and suspicion of strangers; an acquaintance with one manufacturer effectually debars one from connection with a second in the same business. It is with difficulty one is admitted to see their works.... The dress of the people here savours not much of the London mode in general; the people are remarkable for coarseness of feature, and the language is unintelligible.

Mr. Curwen was but the first of an army of writers who have spent as short a time as possible in Manchester and then committed their unfavourable impressions to paper. Poor fellow, he obviously met all the wrong people. Much was going on of which he was unaware.

For instance, the town already had a weekly newspaper, the *Mercury*, published since 3rd March 1752, by Joseph Harrop, its type "so small as to be a trial". It already had a bank, the Manchester Bank, with an office of insurance from fire, opened in December 1771 in St. Ann's Square. The first volume of Whitaker's *History of Manchester* (a thoroughly unreliable book, be it said) appeared in 1770, and in 1772 a *Manchester Directory* of sixty pages, containing the names of 1,150 people and firms engaged in trade. A subscription "library for promoting general knowledge" at 6s. a year was founded in 1770. The town already had a fire brigade. It promoted and paid for its own census in 1773-4. And in 1775 a public fund was launched to raise money "in order to render some of the narrow streets and passages more convenient". Within fourteen days £8,000 was subscribed, and after four months the fund totalled £10,771. As a result Exchange Street was built, Market Place widened, and many other improvements made. This shows a sense of civic pride. Nor was it all.

In 1777 a concert room was built in Fountain Street, the beginning of the famous Gentlemen's Concerts. For some years past a group of enthusiastic flautists had met at a coffee house to give concerts. In 1775 the first Theatre Royal opened, at the corner of Spring Gardens and York Street. Between these two events, in 1776, the Grammar School was rebuilt with two storeys. The intellectuals of the town gathered often in the King Street home of the scholar and scientist Dr. Thomas Percival, and these meetings were given official status in February 1781 with the foundation of the Literary and Philosophical Society (the 'Lit. and Phil.'). It met for twenty-three years in public houses until its headquarters in George Street was built. A paper read by Dr. Thomas Barnes in 1782 shows an early concern for the workers' condition, though he was a voice crying in the wilderness. There should, he said, be an institute of chemistry and mechanics, with a museum containing working models of textile machinery. He was forty years ahead of his time. "The poor", he said, "are the strength and riches of every state. . . . The interest of the poor therefore must, with every considerate man, be the object of his regards." Well, at least a Sunday School had been built off London Road in 1781 where children, who were at work the other days of the week, were taught to read and write. In September 1786 Manchester New College, which grew out of the defunct Warrington Academy, opened its doors in a building in Mosley Street between Bond Street (Princess Street) and St. Peter's Square. Its aim was to promote a "high standard in civil and commercial education".

If all this development is proof of a spirit of enterprise how, it may be asked, notwithstanding the commercial considerations already mentioned, was the feudal local government system tolerated? How could men who formed a literary and philosophical society and a technical college and, in 1790, a lying-in hospital, continue to put up with a Court Leet of the lord of the manor which met only twice a year and with its unpaid officials— the boroughreeve (a powerless mayor), the day police, the scavengers and other feudal survivals? It was probably felt that any new system would not necessarily be more efficient and might be detrimental.

But men of reforming zeal had at least in 1765 set up the Cleansing and Lighting Commissioners. Nearly thirty years later, in 1792, the rapid expansion of the town had brought new difficulties. Water for cleansing was scarce; extra horse traffic made disposal of manure a problem, and the rise in population brought an urgent need for better methods of getting rid of excreta. A special Act of Parliament established the Manchester and Salford Police Commissioners with powers to build drains and sewers and to levy a rate of up to 18d. in the pound. At first they made little use of their authority but at the turn of the century, when the German merchant Brandt became boroughreeve and treasurer, they became more vigorous and efficient. By 1816 they had supplied gas for street and private lighting and used the gasworks profits to offset other municipal costs.

Symbolic of the better aspect of Manchester at this period was the foundation of the Portico Library, which opened in 1806, having cost over £7,000. It has extra significance because it survives to this day, and its building in Mosley Street is the first of the many fine buildings erected in 'modern' Manchester. Apart from the library at Chetham's Hospital School, Manchester had three libraries at the end of the eighteenth century: the Old Subscription Library, dating back to 1765 when its catalogue listed 400 books; the subscription library for promoting general knowledge, founded in 1770 in Fountain Street; and the New Subscription Library opened in 1792 under the impetus of radical ideals from France and regarded as 'dangerous' by the magistrates of Napoleonic times.

The Portico Library was the brainchild of two businessmen, Robert Robinson and Michael Ward, who visited Liverpool in 1796 and were impressed by the Lyceum Library there. Why, they wondered, could Manchester not have a similar institution "uniting the advantages of a news-room and library on an extensive and liberal plan"? The significant point here is the news-room, because it was felt that the businessmen of the town, while they might not be great readers, would patronise a library where they could consult the London and local papers in order to study trade figures and prospects, especially while the wars with France continued.

Robinson and Ward met several initial difficulties, the chief of them, no one will be surprised to hear, being unwillingness to subscribe money. It was to be a proprietary library—owned by its members, each of whom bought a share—with a limited membership of 400. By the middle of 1802 enough money had been collected to justify formation of a committee and appointment of an architect. Their choice was Thomas Harrison (1744–1829), "a man of great modesty and diffidence", one of the first British architects in the neo-classical school. The taste of the time was for imitation of the great buildings of the Greek and Roman ascendancy or of the Italian Renaissance—new buildings were supposed to look like old ones. Harrison had in 1788 designed Chester Castle, with its Doric portico, and had built the single-span Grosvenor Bridge in the same city. Now for his first Manchester commission he designed what may be claimed as the first of the country's classical-revival buildings. He deliberately based it on the Ionic temple of Athene Palias at Priene, adapting and simplifying his model to suit his requirements.

Built in yellow Runcorn stone, the Portico has four unfluted columns on the Mosley Street front, with extra ones along the side in Charlotte Street with windows fitted in between them. In its original form the interior must have been very striking. The

building was roofed by a saucer dome built of timber and inset
with glazed lights and supported by segmental barrel vaults at
each end and segmented arches at the sides. Around the dome, at
gallery level, was the library itself. The whole of the ground floor
was the news-room, lit at first by candles, later by oil, where
"coffee, soups, and other refreshments excepting spirituous
liquors, wines and malt liquor" could be obtained. In the news-
room in 1806 you could have read most of the British newspapers
of the day which included *The Times*, *Morning Chronicle*, *Morning
Post*, *Observer*, *Bell's Weekly Messenger*, *Lloyd's List*, *Gore's Liverpool General Advertiser*, the *Hull Packet*, the *Clyde Commercial
Advertiser* and the three Manchester papers, *Wheeler's*, *Harrop's*
and *Cowdroy's*. Also obtained for the 'proprietors' were the *New
Statesman*, the *Edinburgh Review*, the *Navy List* and many others. A
full-time librarian was appointed. The library's chairman for
thirty-five years from 1849–84 was the Reverend William Gaskell,
Minister of Cross Street Chapel and husband of Elizabeth
Gaskell, the novelist. Thomas de Quincey, a Mancunian, used
the library, and its first secretary (for two years, until he went
to work in London) was a doctor at Manchester Royal Infirmary,
Peter Mark Roget, later to become the compiler of *Roget's
Thesaurus*.

The first committee and subscribers of the Portico Library set
the pattern for many Mancunian enterprises in later years, being
a mixture of professional and business interests. Charles F.
Brandt, the German whom we have met several times already,
was on the committee, so were two members of the Heywood
banking family. There were several doctors and some clergymen,
the rest being 'businessmen'. As an honorary member it had the
most distinguished Mancunian of his day, Dr. John Dalton,
secretary of the 'Lit. and Phil.' and working at this time on his
theory that the atom was the smallest imaginable particle of
matter. He lived in Faulkner Street, behind the Portico, and was
a conspicuous figure in the town, in Quaker dress with knee
breeches, buckled shoes, black hat and carrying a silver-knobbed
stick. Dalton was given free admission to the library in consideration of his undertaking "to superintend the going of the
clock".

In Mosley Street today the refined delicacy of the Portico
building seems an unlikely but charming survival, dwarfed by its

modern office block neighbour on the opposite corner of Charlotte Street. The buses and cars roar past up to Piccadilly, Lewis's is
half a minute's walk away, above its elegant roof you can see the
twentieth-century inelegance of the Piccadilly Plaza. A little
further down the street is the City Art Gallery, but that building
was not there in 1806. Then there were still private houses in
Mosley Street. At its lower end stood St. Peter's Church, conse-
crated in 1794, amid fields and near to the River Tib. Another
new building, at the corner of Princess Street, was the Academy
already mentioned, where Dalton had been Professor of mathematics and natural philosophy from 1793–99 and where he
published his study of colour blindness. Next to the Portico was a
chapel and opposite were the Assembly Rooms, opened in 1792.

Think, when next you pass the Portico Library, that in 1814, to
celebrate Napoleon's banishment to Elba, its front was illuminated
"with coloured lamps". Its kitchens were used in 1830 for a
dinner to the Duke of Wellington when the Manchester-
Liverpool railway was opened, and in 1836 Manchester un-
expectedly staged a music festival at which the principal attraction
was the appearance of Maria Malibran, the most celebrated
mezzo-soprano of her time, enjoying a celebrity comparable with
that of a later Maria, Madame Callas. Unfortunately Malibran
had had an accident in the hunting field a few days earlier and was
taken ill during one of the concerts, dying at the Mosley Arms
Hotel in Piccadilly, at the age of 29.

The Portico has survived many financial crises and many
changes. It has had to sell many of its most valuable books, and in
1920 the news-room was leased to the Bank of Athens and today
is leased to Lloyds Bank. This entailed the despoliation of the
interior by the insertion at gallery level of ugly lay-lights and the
construction of a glass roof to the bank quarters. It also deprived
members of their imposing front entrance. Today they enter by
the side in Charlotte Street, the entrance formerly used by
footmen or servants who called to collect their employers' books.

But if you ascend the narrow staircase, which smells of a
curious mixture of disinfectant and age, you will enter the library
and step out of the feverish activity of the modern city into the
atmosphere and quiet of Victorian Manchester, slightly shabby
but friendly and comfortable. Today the Portico is also a picture
gallery, its members enjoy the best lending library of up-to-date

books in the district, and you can settle into a chair, have a light meal and read or talk, with the shelves of old books, dusty and not much looked at nowadays, as an antiquarian background. But do not imagine that the members are antiquarian too. Today the Portico attracts an increasing number of the younger generation of Mancunians. Solicitors, accountants, barristers, journalists, radio and television people, and businessmen have discovered in the Portico a civilised club with a unique atmosphere in which to meet, talk, argue and settle the affairs of the world, to discuss last night's Hallé concert or United's form last Saturday. To describe them as 'the Portico Set' would not be particularly welcomed, but it would not be inaccurate.

The Portico, then, was the first manifestation in bricks and mortar of the growth of nineteenth-century Manchester. It was quickly followed by others, the second Theatre Royal in Fountain Street among them. Thomas Harrison was also the architect of the second Exchange, which he was invited in 1805 to design. It was opened in 1809. It stood at the corner of Market Street and had a semi-circular frontage. Contemporary engravings show the narrow entrance to St. Ann's Square, with St. Ann's Church in the background. Within thirty years of its opening the subscribers were complaining of the lack of accommodation, so fast was the city still growing—its population in 1821 was 108,016, an increase in ten years of 28,500. The best time for seeing 'high Change' was on a Tuesday, market day, when, said a writer in 1839, "a spectacle will present itself to the visitor that cannot fail to excite ideas in his mind of the magnitude of the business transactions of Manchester merchants and the rapidity with which they appear to dispose of them".

Another disciple of the classical revival in architecture was commissioned to give Manchester its first town hall, in King Street at the corner of Cross Street, where Lloyds Bank stands today. He was Francis Goodwin (1784–1835) and he designed another classical building, with a façade of four Ionic columns and a high parapet with panels in bas-relief. It cost £40,000 and was started in 1822. Its central room was 130 feet by 38 feet, and was decorated by Augustine Aglio in an ornate manner. Britannia was shown overthrowing Napoleon, Lord Macartney was shown meeting the Emperor of China, and the King of Persia was shown receiving an English trade delegation. The building was demolished in 1911, but its central façade was preserved and can be seen in Heaton Park.

Goodwin also designed St. George's Church, Chester Road, Hulme, which is passed daily by thousands of motorists who probably never give it a glance as they prepare to cross the Mancunian Way flyover or negotiate the roundabout near the weed-grown churchyard. This sombre blackened church was built in 1826 in an English medieval style. Its battlemented parapets, its plethora of crockets and pinnacles and buttresses are a depressing sight. Yet they represent the architect's positive revolt against Georgian architecture, which he thought was dull and insipid. He called Wren "a wretched bungler".

Goodwin's one-time partner, Richard Lane, also contributed his quota towards ugly Manchester buildings which are quite unfairly blamed by the unknowing on the Victorian age. The extraordinary Deaf and Dumb School and Blind Asylum (Henshaw's Institute) at Old Trafford, for example, built in 1834, is like some Gothic nightmare, a town house for Dracula. Lane is better represented to today's Mancunians by his Salford Town Hall (1825) in the classical style, the Friends' Meeting House in Mount Street (1828), Chorlton-on-Medlock Town Hall (1830) and Stockport Infirmary (1832). Less admirable were the Corn Exchange at Hanging Ditch and the Union Club in Mosley Street.

Regency Manchester, too, gave first opportunities to Charles Barry, architect of the Houses of Parliament. In 1822, when he was 27, he was recommended by Sir John Soane as architect for All Saints Church, Prestwich. In the same year he also designed St. Matthew, Campfield (demolished in 1951). In 1824 he won a competition for the building of the Royal Manchester Institution, Mosley Street, built at a cost of over £30,000 as the headquarters of the institution which was founded in 1823 to encourage literature, science and the arts. Every three years it held an art exhibition to which the landed gentry lent their old masters. Today this building is the City Art Gallery, dreadfully inadequate for its purpose, but still noble to look at. The art gallery annexe is now in the Athenaeum, also designed by Barry in 1836 after he had won the competition for the Houses of Parliament. It was the first Manchester building in the imitation Italian Renaissance style which was to be the feature of the next twenty years'

architectural development in the town. The Athenaeum was
originally a library and lecture-room "for the middle classes".
Franz Liszt played there.

These were the outward and visible symbols of a thriving
community, brimming with self-confidence. There were others.
The manufacturers formed, in 1820, a Chamber of Commerce to
promote and protect their interests. In 1821 Market Street and
other streets were widened and improved. In the same year
eleven middle-class Radicals put up £1,050 between them to
found a weekly newspaper to express their views. Their idea was
to provide a forum for a young cotton merchant, John Edward
Taylor, who had made a name as a writer at the time of Peterloo
two years earlier. So, with Taylor as editor, the *Manchester
Guardian* first appeared on 5th May 1821, price 7d. It was a
success, and he repaid his sponsors, with interest, in three years.
The paper introduced a new feature into the town's journalism,
the leading article. Also, none of the other papers had a reporter.
Jeremiah Garnett was the first *Manchester Guardian* reporter (and
its editor from 1848–61). In 1818 the Savings Bank, for the
working classes, was established in King Street; there were over
100 Sunday Schools in Manchester and Salford by this date; a
waterworks company was formed; in 1825 the Manchester
Mechanics' Institution was opened in a £7,000 building in
Cooper Street, thanks largely to the beneficence of the banker Sir
Benjamin Heywood—its objects were to give instruction in the
trades they practised to the working classes, as well as in "other
branches of useful knowledge, *excluding* party politics and
controversial theology". For 5s. a quarter the working-man could
have access to what today would be called adult, or further,
education.

In 1830 there was a major development in the industrial and
commercial life of the town and its region: the railways came to
Manchester. The Stockton and Darlington Railway had opened
in 1825 but a project for a Liverpool and Manchester link had
been discussed in 1822. The delays experienced by traders in
sending goods by canal—especially during winter frosts—led a
number of businessmen to explore the advantages of the new,
faster mode of travel and a public company was formed in 1824
with a share capital of £400,000. An attempt to get a Bill through
Parliament—Manchester not being represented there, it should be

remembered, until 1832—failed in 1825 but was successful the following year. George Stephenson was appointed chief engineer to the company.

The first major feats of construction were the draining of Chat Moss, the swamp across which the line had to run, the boring of the Liverpool tunnel, and the construction of the Sankey viaduct —nine arches each of 50-foot span—to take the railway nearly 70 feet over the Sankey canal. The railway approached Manchester past Worsley Hall, by bridge over the Worsley canal, through Eccles and past "several country seats and villas whose rich lawns and flourishing plantations afford an agreeable variety", over the Irwell at Salford and into the station at Liverpool Road. The line was opened on 15th September 1830 in the presence of the Duke of Wellington, the occasion being marred by the death of William Huskisson, an able Cabinet Minister and early supporter of the company, who was struck by Stephenson's 'Rocket' at Parkside, near Newton-le-Willows.

Liverpool Road remained the terminus until 1844, when the line was extended to the new Victoria Station to join the Manchester-Leeds railway. The station had purposely been sited in open fields, with a view of Hulme Hall and a bowling green near by. It is preserved today as an historic relic. Manchester was linked with London in 1842 with a line through Stockport and Crewe, and to Sheffield, through the Woodhead Tunnel, in 1845.

It hardly needs stressing how these new lines of communication benefited Manchester economically. What perhaps does need stressing is the almost evangelical fervour with which the new invention was greeted by those who pioneered it. We can catch its authentic flavour in the last pages of the book about the construction of the Liverpool-Manchester line written in 1830 by the company's treasurer, Henry Booth. After expounding the commercial advantages to employer and employed, advantages "with all the indications of health, energy and cheerfulness", he continued:

> But perhaps the most striking result produced by the completion of this railway is the sudden and marvellous change which has been effected in our ideas of time and space. Notions which we have received from our ancestors and verified by our own experience are overthrown in a day and a new standard erected by which to form our ideas for the future. Speed—despatch—distance—are still

relative terms, but their meaning has changed within a few months: what was quick is now slow; what was distant is now near; and this change in our ideas will not be limited to the environs of Liverpool and Manchester—it will pervade society at large. . . . What a revolution in the whole system and detail of business, when the ordinary rate of travelling shall be twenty miles, instead of ten, per hour. . . . The man of business in Manchester will breakfast at home, proceed to Liverpool by the railway, transact his business, and return to Manchester before dinner. A hard day's journeying is thus converted into a morning's excursion.

And this was his not unworthy peroration:

The spirit of the times must needs manifest itself in the progress of events, and the movement is too impetuous to be stayed, were it wise to attempt it. Like the "Rocket" of fire and steam, or its prototype of war and desolation—whether the harbinger of peace and the arts, or the Engine of hostile attack and devastation—though it be a futile attempt to oppose so mighty an impulse, it may not be unworthy our ambition to guide its progress and direct its course.

Progress in travel, building and good works. But what of the residents of the town? In that respect Manchester lagged and the truth has to be faced that residentially, because of its swift expansion, it was jerry-built. Already, by 1837, could be seen the contrasts of prosperity and poverty. No Georgian architect left to Manchester a legacy comparable with the residential developments at Edinburgh, Buxton, Newcastle upon Tyne and Liverpool. A few houses in St. John Street, the Crescent at Salford, some houses in King Street and in the village of Ardwick Green. That was all. The rest was cheap and insanitary.

Already a most important change was occurring. Houses were being left empty as their former owners found houses outside the city. They were pulled down and factories and warehouses put up in their place. In 1820 Manchester had 126 warehouses; nine years later it had more than 1,000. A guide to Manchester published in 1839 notes that

within the last few years Mosley Street contained only private dwelling-houses: it is now converted almost entirely into warehouses; and the increasing business of the town is rapidly converting all the principal dwelling-houses which exist in that neighbourhood into mercantile establishments and is driving most of the respectable inhabitants into the suburbs.

In 1837 Eccles was a country suburb, Chorlton-on-Medlock was considered the rival of the best London suburbs, Ardwick Green had a lake surrounded by handsome dwellings, part of Hulme was a village among trees and fields. The reign of Queen Victoria was signalled by the beginning of Victoria Park, 2 miles outside Manchester, at Rusholme, and opened on 31st July 1837. Here on 140 acres "a company of gentlemen" had formed a company "to build villa houses at rents varying from £100 to £250 a year" within a ringed fence and guarded by a toll-gate. The park contained 5 miles of roads, laid out in crescents and terraces, with ornamental shrubs, trees and flowers. It combined, as a contemporary chronicler said, "the advantage of a close proximity to the town, the privacy and advantage of a country residence which, in the rapid conversion of all the former private residences of the town into warehouses, has long been deemed to be a desideratum".

This was where for years the élite of Manchester were to live. They chose it, in the first place, for one very practical reason which is the basic reason why people left Manchester. It was not only a case of property becoming warehouses. It was in order to escape the dense pall of smoke from the factory chimneys which covered the town and all its buildings in filth and through which the sun shone, as de Tocqueville said, like a disc without rays. The rape of Manchester by the Industrial Revolution had long been accomplished. It is time to turn away from the Greek porticos and Italian façades to look at the other side of the picture which resulted from the trade of the town; to look not only at the elegance of the Portico Library and the opulence of the Old Town Hall but at the "narrow and loathsome streets, and close courts, defiled with refuse" and at what Robert Southey as early as 1802 called the hotbeds of infection where the poor lived.

1806 oasis in Mosley Street, the Portico Library

FOUR

"...AND ON THIS"

HAD I been writing this book a few years ago, it would have been inevitable that I should have depicted Manchester as it broke upon the vision of the train traveller, who, on leaving Stockport, could watch a panorama of industrial gloom and squalor, with the roofs of rows of mean houses piled street upon street, chimneys, drab back gardens, all confirming the worst fears and illusions held about the city by any stranger. No approach to a city by train is very seductive, and usually confirms the belief that man's ugliest invention is corrugated iron. But the journey into London Road, as it then was, from Stockport was especially depressing, unless one cherishes a Betjemanesque affection and admiration for the railway viaduct. H. S. Gibbs, in his *Autobiography of a Manchester Cotton Manufacturer*, published in 1887, recalled his arrival by rail from Bristol in February 1850:

> It was not until I had reached Stockport, and was crossing the viaduct, which affords a comprehensive view of that town, that I began to realise the great change in my life about to take place. There were the mills beneath me, of which I had heard so much, and gloomy structures they appeared; and it must have been the time for "firing up" with most of them, as there was scarcely a chimney visible which did not appear to be doing heavy duty.

The journey from Stockport today is still no prospect of beauty, but on both sides the old order is being swept away; and as one rounds the corner into Piccadilly one can catch a glimpse of the new Manchester—no smoke, no belching chimneys, in their place tall buildings, white and glassy, and on the left a view of the high flats that have replaced the hideous remains of the years of wealth-begotten poverty. This new city has been a long

St Peter's Square and the Central Library

time coming, but slowly and steadily it is materialising. Everywhere are the ubiquitous bulldozer, the cleared site, the hoardings enclosing the foundations of new buildings. There are many harsh things to be said about Manchester's civic administrators, but there is no denying that someone in the Town Hall has stubbornly kept faith with the belief that a modern and impressive, even a beautiful, city might one day stand on the site of the old commercial Babylon. There is still a long way to go, still too many people living in disgraceful surroundings, but the dream is capable of realisation: that much, unbelievable a few years ago, is now apparent. How brave a dream it was in the first place can only be appreciated if Thomas Hardy's wise words from "In Tenebris" are heeded: "If way to the Better there be, it exacts a full look at the Worst."

Lord Torrington visited Manchester in 1790. After breakfast at the 'Bridgewater Arms' he wandered about "this great nasty manufacturing town. . . . Who but a merchant could live in such a hole where the slave working and drinking a short life out is eternally reeling before you from fatigue or drunkenness?" Twelve years later the poet Robert Southey visited the town:

> The dwellings of the labouring manufacturers are in narrow streets and lanes crowded together because every inch of land is of such value that room for light and air cannot be afforded them. Here in Manchester a great proportion of the poor lodge in cellars damp and dark, where every kind of filth is suffered to accumulate, because no exertions of domestic care can ever make such homes decent. . . . Imagine this multitude crowded together in narrow streets, the houses all built of brick and blackened with smoke; frequent large buildings among them where you hear from within the everlasting din of machinery and where when the bell rings it is to call wretches to their work instead of to their prayers. Imagine this and you have the materials of a picture of Manchester.

The Industrial Revolution soon did its dirty work. By 1789 a woman visitor to Manchester could write in her diary: "Manchester is a Dull, Smoky, Dirty Town in a Flat, from whence the Black Soot rises in clouds to Overspread the surrounding Country." It was in the streets surrounding the Collegiate Church, the Old Town, that most of the workers lived in conditions that would be unimaginable had they not been so accurately and devastatingly recorded.

Epidemics of fever were common and lethal. John Ferriar, a physician at the Infirmary, investigated the poor districts and reported to the Police Commissioners that "the horror of those houses cannot easily be described; a lodger fresh from the country often lies down in a bed, filled with infection by its last tenant, or from which the corpse of a victim to fever has only been removed a few hours before". Ferriar proposed the licensing and regular inspection of all lodging houses, provision of nurses and proper ventilation of factories. He and some colleagues organised the town's first public health service and opened a fever hospital (in Portland Street) optimistically called the House of Recovery because it met opposition from patients' relatives who objected to their loved ones being taken from home to die.

Other men with social consciences were appalled by what they saw and tried to alleviate the sufferings of the workers. Peter Drinkwater, owner of a mill in what is now Aytoun Street, did his best to provide decent lavatories for his employees, and he was fortunate in his manager, Robert Owen, later to found New Lanark and to pioneer a new style of management-worker relations. But little enough generally was done. A new poorhouse was built in Strangeways in 1792 where the poor might be punished for misconduct by confinement, starvation or hard labour.

Children went to work in the mills for thirteen hours a day, deprived of education, exercise, fresh air and sleep. Stunted growth, deformities and other physical defects caused by dreadful conditions, malnutrition and the filthy atmosphere of street, home and mill were common in Lancashire until not many years ago. (As a child in Eccles in the 1930s I remember being frightened by seeing deformed and stunted men and women in the streets.) The growth of population effectively negatived any kind of relief work; the rapid influx of Irish was a particularly pressing problem. Between 1821 and 1831 the population increased by 45 per cent, the 'immigrants' moving into houses vacated by those who could afford to live outside the town. In May 1832 cholera reached Manchester and raged until December. Of the population of 142,000, just over 670 died of the disease. A board of health was formed with Dr. James Kay as secretary and he published a report on the "moral and physical condition of the working classes" in the cotton industry, which was one of the earliest and most thorough of social surveys. Kay inspected 6,951 houses and found, among other things, that 6,565 of them urgently needed white-washing of the interior, 1,435 were damp and 2,221 were without privies. Of 687 streets, 248 were unpaved and 352 contained pools, heaps of debris, refuse and dung.

Another doctor, a physician named Carus in the suite of the King of Saxony was in Manchester in 1844. He noticed the "pallid population" and the "practical utility of the buildings" and also that

> everyone of any property has a country house at some distance from the town and only enters its atmosphere of smoke when his presence there is absolutely necessary. . . . I could not help being forcibly struck by the peculiar dense atmosphere which hangs over these towns in which hundreds of chimneys are continually vomiting forth clouds of smoke. The light even is quite different from what it is elsewhere.

Carus was one of three important foreign visitors during 1844, a sign of the importance Manchester had reached in foreign eyes: it was the exciting and 'significant' city of the age, and it attracted visitors, especially literary ones, like flies. The other visitors were a Frenchman, Léon Faucher, and a German, Frederick Engels. Both wrote books about Manchester, which, though details can be challenged and certain emphases quibbled over, are in essence an invaluable and unanswerable indictment of the social conditions.

Faucher dealt with a subject from which most English observers averted their gaze. He asserted that if you passed the Exchange towards dusk you would be sure to meet over 500 prostitutes. In Manchester in 1843 were 330 brothels containing 701 prostitutes, according to the police report, but large numbers of 'amateurs' among the mill-workers added to their poor wages by the fruits of prostitution. And in the many trade depressions when mills were closed there was an enormous increase in the numbers resorting to prostitution. 'Factory girl' was a term of abuse; there was nothing of the warm and friendly Gracie Fields implication in the term in the mid-nineteenth century.

> The factory girls (says Faucher in his *Manchester in 1844*) are strangers to modesty. Their language is gross and often obscene; and when they do not marry early, they form illicit connections which

degrade them still more than premature marriage. It is a common occurrence to meet in the intervals of labour, in the back streets, couples of males and females which the caprice of the moment has brought together.

The results in venereal disease hardly need stressing.

Drunkenness also contributed its share to the moral decline. Apart from gin and whiskey dispensed from the illicit stills of the Irish, beer was the favourite drink. In 1843 Manchester possessed 920 retailers of beer, 624 public-houses and thirty-one inns and hotels. Faucher quotes an observer who, in forty minutes, saw 112 men and 163 women enter a tavern, the women being worse than the men in their craving for liquor. The taverns were open as early as 5 a.m. and closed late at night and many manufacturers distributed wages in public-houses on a Saturday night. "Is it not thus", Faucher asked, "that the ancients degraded their slaves, from fear lest, their reason being developed, they should aspire to liberty?"

The worst debauchery occurred at weekends. Sunday was as bad as Saturday. The Victorian Sunday found the middle-class at church, but the depressingly sombre presentation of religion made no appeal to the poor. Methodism's puritanical aspect was repellent to many, as Scotland proved above anywhere else. So when the church services were over and the pubs opened, the working-class flocked back into them. Where else could they go in 1844? There were no parks, no avenues, not even a public common. The roads were dusty and poorly maintained. Everything in the suburbs was private property—trespassers will be prosecuted. The Botanical Gardens,* even the cemeteries, were closed. The effects of the sudden industrialisation of English life have never been more movingly analysed than by a mechanic named Titus Rowbotham who, at the age of 51, made a deposition to a committee of manufacturers:

> When I came to Manchester in 1801 the operatives, like myself, were better fed, better clothed, more moral, and of a more vigorous

* The Botanical Gardens were at Old Trafford, on Stretford Road. Before choosing this site the directors, anxious to avoid smoke, asked John Dalton for advice. He provided them with the records he had kept for forty years showing the direction of the wind. These showed that for seven-tenths of the year the gardens would be free from wind-blown deposits from the direction of the town.

constitution. The children that are born now are a race much more
feeble than their parents. . . . I have the most lively recollection of
what passed in my youth. I have before my eyes the images of those
who are now dead as distinctly as though they yet lived. The men
that I see now do not at all resemble them. . . . Their intellect is
enfeebled and withered like a tree. They are more like grown up
children than the race of men I knew formerly. I know many
instances of operatives who had, in their youth, the reputation of
considerable intelligence, but which has decayed and soon become
extinct with the advance of years; and yet these men are younger
than I. The long hours of labour, and the high temperature of the
factories, produce lassitude and excessive exhaustion. The operatives
cannot eat and seek to sustain life by the excitement of drink.

Even more remarkable than Faucher's book is Engels's *The
Condition of the Working Class in England*, published in Leipzig in
1845 when its author was only 25. It is, of course, a corner-stone
of Marxism, but politics hardly enter into our acceptance today of
his documentation of what he saw in Manchester when he went
there in 1842 as manager of the English branch of his father's
cotton firm, Ermen and Engels, of Barmen. He describes how, by
this date, the 'conurbation' had developed as a girdle of towns
round the central town. He shrewdly points out that the town
was

peculiarly built, so that a person may live in it for years, and go in
and out daily without coming into contact with a working-people's
quarter or even with workers, that is, so long as he confines himself
to his business or to pleasure walks. This arises chiefly from the fact
that, by unconscious tacit agreement, as well as with outspoken
conscious determination, the working-people's quarters are sharply
separated from the sections of the city reserved for the middle-class.

Except for the commercial district, all Manchester, Engels said,
all Salford and Hulme, a great part of Pendleton and Chorlton-
on-Medlock, two-thirds of Ardwick and single stretches of
Broughton and Cheetham Hill were working-class districts. This
was the "girdle of squalor". Beyond this lived "the upper and
middle class bourgeoisie", the former

in remoter villas with gardens in Chorlton and Ardwick, or on the
breezy heights of Cheetham Hill, Broughton and Pendleton in free,
wholesome country air, in fine, comfortable houses . . . . and the
finest part of this arrangement is that the members of this money

aristocracy can take the shortest road through the middle of all the
labouring districts to their places of business without ever seeing that
they are in the midst of the grimy misery that lurks to the right and
left. For the thoroughfares leading from the Exchange in all directions
out of the city are lined, on both sides, with an almost unbroken
series of shops . . . which, out of self-interest, care for a decent and
cleanly external appearance.

In fact, the place was a whited sepulchre, only it was black.

Engels's descriptions of the slums of Manchester are famous, but
no portrait of the city would be complete without some quotation
from them, if only as a reminder to the present generation of how
fortunate they are to live in a 'welfare state', which, whatever its
inequalities and shortcomings, would have seemed like the New
Jerusalem to those dwellers in the Long Millgate area on the
banks of the Irk less than 150 years ago:

> In one of these courts there stands directly at the entrance, at the
> end of the covered passage, a privy without a door, so dirty that the
> inhabitants can pass into and out of the court only by passing through
> foul pools of stagnant urine and excrement. . . . He who turns to the
> left from the main street, Long Millgate, is lost; he wanders from one
> court to another, turns countless corners, passes nothing but narrow,
> filthy nooks and alleys, until after a few minutes he has lost all
> clue. . . . Everywhere heaps of débris, refuse and offal; standing
> pools for gutters, and a stench which alone would make it impossible
> for a human being in any degree civilised to live in such a district.

Manchester's "most horrible spot", according to Engels, was
'Little Ireland', south-west of Oxford Road near the Medlock—
"the race that lives in these ruinous cottages, behind broken
windows mended with oilskin, sprung doors, and rotten door-
posts, or in dark wet cellars, in measureless filth and stench, this
race must really have reached the lowest stage of humanity".
Hulme and Ancoats were equally condemned, and also the
working-class district which stretched on both sides of Deansgate:

> especially in the immediate vicinity of the business quarter, between
> Bridge and Quay Streets, Princess and Peter Streets, the crowded
> construction exceeds in places the narrowest courts of the Old
> Town. . . . According to Dr. Kay the most demoralised class of all
> Manchester lived in these ruinous and filthy districts, people whose

occupations are thieving and prostitution; and, to all appearance, his assertion is still true. . . .

And Salford, Engels said, was even worse.

Horrible as conditions were in succeeding years, this 1840 period probably represented the nadir of Manchester's degradation. The Irwell, in which salmon had once flourished, had as late as 1819 still contained gudgeon, and at Albert Bridge, Salford, swallows and house martins flashed above its surface, but within a year or two it became a stagnant, filthy, vile-smelling stream, an open sewer, its surface covered with gas tar, every kind of refuse and scum emptied into it from the mills and warehouses from the towns along its banks. The Medlock, too, was similarly polluted.

Other British towns and cities at this period housed equally fearful conditions, some even worse, notably London, Liverpool and Glasgow. This was the aftermath of Regency England, and its moral debauchery ran alongside its industrialisation. The gin palaces and brothels familiar from George Cruikshank's drawings were not confined to the metropolis. In spite of Engels's predictable assault on 'the bourgeoisie', not everyone was indifferent to the condition of the working-class, nor was Engels the only man to walk past the shop-fronts of Market Street to see what lay beyond. The originals of Dickens's Cheeryble Brothers were in business in the city at the beginning of the nineteenth century, William and Daniel Grant, with a warehouse in Cannon Street.

Much scorn is poured on the Victorian age, on its hypocrisy, smugness and piety, but this too must be remembered: that it inherited the vile legacy of too swift industrialisation and the consequent over-rapid expansion of populations in towns which, like Manchester, still had no proper system of municipal government to enable them to cope with the transformation and its attendant problems. It inherited this, and it began to do something about it, slowly, inadequately and primitively, no doubt, by modern standards, but nonetheless something was done. Social workers, the church, temperance societies—all contributed towards making the life of the poor more tolerable.

The worst of the slums were swept away—'Little Ireland', for example—although others took their place. But in those slums grew a race of people who do not merit the kind of description Engels had perforce to apply to the sub-human dwellers in sub-human dwellings. Thousands of dignified lives were lived in Ancoats and Hulme, lives of self-improvement, of sacrifice to give children a chance of education, lives of genuine piety and sincerely-held religious beliefs, unrecorded but good lives by good people with an innate Lancashire pride in the home.

Nor must it be thought by a modern generation fed upon plays of Lancashire life as interpreted by Granada Television that all employers were wicked exploiters of labour. No doubt at all but that many of them were—there are good and bad employers now, as then. But men such as Robert Greg, the Ashworth brothers, Grant, Ashton and Strutt set, in the 1830s and earlier, a first example of benevolent employment, providing medical super-vision, day schools for infants, evening and Sunday schools for children, and special working clothes for the women. (Yet Greg saw nothing wrong in expecting children to attend school for two hours after a twelve-hour working day and in fact declared that they enjoyed it. Better this, though, than the fate of $7\frac{1}{2}$-year-old Thomas Price, 'a climbing boy', who died in 1847 from the combined effects of ill-usage from his master and suffocation and burns received while cleaning a flue in Jackson Street, Chorlton-on-Medlock.)

Nor was the reading public kept unaware of the prevailing conditions. In 1848 Mrs. Gaskell's *Mary Barton* appeared, a novel based on the close observation of Manchester life she had acquired since her marriage in 1832. Here for almost the first time the results of the Industrial Revolution became the real theme of a novel—I say "almost", because Disraeli's *Sybil*, published in 1845, had used Manchester as a background. But *Mary Barton*, in its contrast of wealth and poverty, was a pioneer study, followed up seven years later by *North and South*, a penetrating account of the various levels of Lancashire life: the employer-employee relation-ship, the strikers, the Irish immigrants, the craving for betterment, the early deaths and simple piety. And in 1854 came Charles Dickens's *Hard Times*, in which 'Coketown' may be taken as Manchester.

In 1844, the year of John Dalton's death, Mosley Street was no longer the "retired residential street" it had been thirty-eight years earlier when he had first crossed it to wind the Portico

Library's clock. Those who once lived there, or their sons, were now in Victoria Park, or in the pleasant village of Didsbury and their former houses had given way to warehouses. The slum clearance that followed 1844 was largely dictated by commercial rather than humanitarian motives: between 1841 and 1851 hundreds of houses off Market Street were pulled down so that warehouses, factories and railway extensions could be built; 600 houses were demolished between 1861 and 1871 in the Piccadilly area for a goods station at London Road and a similar clearance was made in the Deansgate area for warehouses, offices and Central Station. In 1851 about 90,000 people lived in the central area of Manchester. Fifty years later, after the vast commercial expansion of the second half of the century, the number was down to 30,000.

Cotton was not the sole cause of this expansion. In the con- urbation area were steelworks and ironworks, woollen mills around Rochdale, paper mills at Bolton and Bury, hat manu- facture at Stockport, Oldham and Denton. There were railway workshops at Gorton, Longsight and Newton Heath; precision tools and armaments were made by Sir Joseph Whitworth; engineering firms already included names as famous as those of Mather and Platt, Sharp Roberts and Galloways. William Fairbairn's steam engine, bridge-building and boiler works was at Ancoats.

It is no wonder that the bad housing developed so near to the factories. Who in those days would have wanted a long walk to and from work after spending twelve or thirteen hours working in the mill? It was the building of these cheap and dreary workers' houses between 1800 and 1840 that caused the major Mancunian housing problem, the worst being the back-to-back and cellar types. But back-to-back houses were banned by local legislation in Manchester in this crucial year of 1844.

Local legislation brings me to the crux of this chapter: the growth of a better-governed Manchester. The workshop of the world it might have been, but few workshops survive with archaic management. From 1820 onwards moves were made to draw up a charter for Manchester but they met with no success. A group of progressive-minded radicals was becoming increasingly dis- contented with the Police Commissioners. Refuse disposal and provision of paving were in arrears. There was complete lack of co-ordination between the Court Leet, who administered justice, and the Police Commissioners, who were supposed to administer public services. No member of either body was a magistrate. Prominent men became less and less anxious to serve on the Court Leet. Their chance came with the Municipal Reform Act of 1835, which, although it only reformed existing boroughs and did not create any new ones (except Stockport), at least provided for the creation by royal charter of new boroughs with elected councils and separate benches of magistrates if, and only if, enough influential inhabitants petitioned the Crown.

So in Manchester a young Radical, Richard Cobden, with some colleagues, campaigned for an end to feudal government of the town and called upon the boroughreeve to hold a town's meeting in the Town Hall, where a resolution for incorporation was passed. A petition, containing over 15,000 signatures, was submitted to the Privy Council in March 1838. In October the charter was received constituting Manchester a municipal borough with an area of just under 4,300 acres, including Chorlton-on-Medlock, Hulme, Ardwick, Beswick and Cheetham, divided into fifteen wards with a council of a mayor, sixteen aldermen and forty-eight councillors. The population was now over 240,000.

If Cobden thought that his battle was won he made a great mistake. The opposition refused to accept defeat, maintaining that the charter was illegal because it had been granted against the wishes of most householders. There followed a deplorable and ridiculous period of municipal guerrilla warfare. The three bodies who opposed the new council—the Police Commissioners, collectors of a police rate; the Overseers and Churchwardens, collectors of a poor rate; and the Surveyors of Highways, who also collected a rate—refused to acknowledge its existence. The charter made no mention of a transfer of powers, so the Commissioners continued as though nothing else had happened. They refused to allow the Town Hall to be used for revision of the voters' list and for the first meeting of the borough council, which therefore had to be held in the York Hotel, King Street, when Thomas Potter became the first mayor, Joseph Heron the town clerk and Cobden an alderman.

Another clash came over the appointment of thirty-one borough magistrates, who were not acknowledged by the overseers. The churchwardens refused to levy the borough rate, and £29,000 had to be guaranteed by supporters of the new council. The council's police force of 343 officers and constables was opposed by the Court Leet's force and the Commissioners' day and night forces. The New Bailey Prison would not admit prisoners committed by borough magistrates unless they were also county magistrates. The borough coroner had a feud with the county coroner and an appeal to the courts about this led to an Act of Parliament in 1842 confirming the charter. The mayor and town clerk went to divine service in this year in the Collegiate Church, the first time they had been recognised by the church-wardens. In this year, too, the Corporation was granted its coat of arms and its motto, 'Concilio et Labore', 'By Planning and Work'. It had earned it.

The final chapters in the democratisation of Manchester were in 1846, when the Court Leet came to an end with the purchase by the Corporation for £200,000 from Sir Oswald Mosley of the lordship of the manor and its associated rights and privileges, and in 1851 when the Corporation bought the waterworks company. There were plans to provide public parks, to buy street-cleaning machines, and to widen and build more streets. Queen Victoria and Prince Albert visited Manchester in October 1851, and on 29th March 1853 the town was created by Royal Charter the City of Manchester.

FIVE

CAPS OF LIBERTY

MANCHESTER'S reputation as a rebellious place, the home of anti-authoritarian, even seditious ideas, dates from the Civil War, when the majority of the 5,000 inhabitants supported Parliament against the Royalists. To subdue Lancashire the King needed to capture Manchester, but the town successfully resisted a siege, thanks largely to preparations for its defence made by Colonel John Rosworm, a German military engineer who had settled there in the Spring of 1642. Lord Strange, later Earl of Derby, had 4,000 infantry, 200 horse and seven guns on the Salford bank of the Irwell on 25th September 1642, but he failed to take the town and withdrew after a week. In 1644 Prince Rupert was at Stockport but by-passed Manchester to capture Bolton and Liverpool.

Plague broke out in the town in 1645, and thereafter the war passed it by. The execution of Charles I and the oppressive Cromwell régime seem to have convinced Mancunians that they were on the wrong side, and, led by the monarchist Warden of the 'owd church', Richard Heyrick, they lent their support henceforward to the Stuart cause. Within a century the town had become a stronghold of the Jacobites. The Mosleys of Ancoats Hall were prominent Jacobites, so were John Byrom and his family.

There is a legend, but no proof, that Prince Charles Edward stayed in the town in 1744 before the '45 rising and that he was 'Mr. Anon' who contributed to the subscription concerts. If he came to spur recruiting he had little success because only 300 men enlisted in his cause and the whole ill-fated, badly organised venture is interesting as far as Manchester is concerned only because the Jacobite song "Farewell Manchester" dates from this

time and because the Prince resided for a brief spell after 29th
November 1745 at John Dickinson's house in Market Street,
which thereafter was nicknamed 'the Palace'. It stood near the
Palace Street of today. He is said to have attended divine service
at the Collegiate Church. Eight leading Manchester Regiment
Jacobites were later executed for treason on Kensington Common,
and in August 1746 the heads of three were placed on spikes on
the Exchange, from which they were stolen five months later.

The history of political disorder in Manchester begins effectively
with the sudden growth of the town outlined in the preceding
two chapters. In 1756 food riots followed the inability of dealers
to supply the needs of the growing populations: food had to be
taken some distance and in the winter the roads were often
impassable. Consequently prices rose. The most serious of the
disturbances was the 'Shudehill Fight' in November 1757, when
dissidents from Ashton-under-Lyne, Oldham and other outlying
towns raided mills and markets during a weekend and were
driven off by soldiers, with some loss of life. The following year
saw what may well have been the first 'strike' in the cotton trade,
when about 10,000 operatives stopped work to demand higher
wages. Whether they were successful is not certainly known,
but at least 1759 marked the end of the long-resented obligation
on all inhabitants of Manchester to grind their corn and malt at
the Lord of the Manor's mill on the Irk. An Act repealed the
ancient custom except where it related to malt.

The first serious disorders in Manchester were occasioned not by
hunger, nor by desire for higher wages, nor by strictly political
motives. They were caused by fear of the machine. Wages in
spinning at this time were in fact high, and agricultural workers
were leaving the land to take better-paid work in the mills.
Machines, their opponents believed, meant fewer jobs. It was in
1779 that Samuel Crompton, of Hall-i'-th'-Wood, near Bolton,
invented the 'mule', a combination of the jenny and the water-
frame; and it was in 1779 that the first riots directed against
spinning machinery occurred. These first signs of the Luddite
campaign caused Manchester employers to 'go easy' on making
immediate use of steam engines. The first steam-driven machinery
in Lancashire cotton factories was at Warrington in 1787. There
was none in Manchester until two years later, when the model
employer Peter Drinkwater installed one in his mill and increased

his production thirtyfold. But when, the next year, Robert Grimshaw of Gorton started a weaving factory at Knott Mill with thirty steam looms he was immediately threatened and a few weeks later the mill was burned to the ground. No other employer used a steam loom in Manchester until sixteen years later, in 1806.

Manchester's real political troubles began on 24th May 1808, when weavers met in St. George's Fields in support of a parliamentary Bill fixing a minimum wage. They met again next day, the Riot Act was read, and soldiers were ordered to disperse the meeting, which they did, killing one man and wounding several. Colonel Thomas Hanson of Strangeways Hall, one of Manchester's most distinguished volunteer corps soldiers, sympathised with the weavers and urged them to disperse, with a promise that their interests would be safeguarded. For this gesture he was arrested, accused of incitement to riot, and sentenced to six months in gaol and a fine of £100. The effect of this prosecution of their friend was to embitter the weavers and goes some way to explaining their mood over the next years. After his release, Hanson gave evidence to the Commons on the weavers' plight in 1811, but later that year he died at the age of 37.

In 1812 there were more food riots: a mob broke into the Exchange and tried to set it on fire. Further Luddite incidents occurred in the mills around Manchester, notably at Middleton and Westhoughton. The end of the war in 1815 brought more distress. England no longer had a monopoly of European markets, and a bad harvest in 1816 and a tax on corn sharply increased the price of food. Riots became the order of the day throughout the country, and the Radicals' movement for reform of the House of Commons, with better representation of the people, began to gather momentum. In Manchester the first Reform meetings were held on St. Peter's Field in the winter of 1816. Not unnaturally the authorities began to be alarmed by the rebellious mood—and before they are condemned utterly as reactionary oppressors let it be remembered that the excesses of the French Revolution were still fresh in the minds of governing authority.

A further St. Peter's Field meeting in the spring of 1817 protested against the suspension a week earlier of the Habeas Corpus Act because of riots in London. Several hundred present at the Manchester meeting decided to march to London to present a petition of protest. Each marcher had a blanket or rug in which to sleep on the way, hence their nickname of the 'Blanketeers'. Some of the leaders were arrested and some of the marchers went as far as Macclesfield before their disorganised action fizzled out in failure. But the very idea of such a march affrighted the authorities in Manchester, who had already been warned by their unpopular deputy constable, Joseph Nadin, that the "lower orders . . . are very clamorous . . . and they talk of a general union throughout the country".

The March of the Blanketeers appeared to the magistrates as "a most daring and traitorous conspiracy the object of which is nothing less than open insurrection and rebellion". It was decided to form a local defence force, the Manchester and Salford Yeomanry, a cavalry group of volunteers from among the town's traders, manufacturers and shopkeepers. Thus were events moving towards 'Peterloo', the most famous and controversial episode in Manchester's history.

No event in history is as cut and dried, as black and white, as some historians make it seem—certainly not Peterloo, the Manchester Massacre. In considering it yet again it must be remembered that the voltage of political feeling was high in 1819. For four years the weavers and other cotton operatives of Manchester and surrounding towns had endured unemployment, high prices for food, low wages (half in 1819 what they were in 1806) and worsening living conditions. There was also discontent with the increasing mechanisation of industry; and because there was often no work, men and women had time to attend meetings at which Radical orators explained to them the indisputable need for parliamentary reform.

Peterloo was also the inevitable result of the anomalous position in which Manchester now found itself and which I have already stressed—a modern manufacturing town governed by feudal laws as though it was still a village. There was then no regular and organised police force. The town's authorities were the county magistrates, whose responsibility it was to disperse mobs within the hour, to read the Riot Act, to enrol special constables and to call in the militia if their aid was needed to maintain law and order. Their principal responsibility was to the property-owners of Manchester, the shopkeepers and traders. And it has to be admitted that they had plenty to alarm them.

The language used in the reformers' speeches and newspapers

The Law Courts in Crown Square

was extremely violent, threatening and provocative. A spinners' strike in 1818 had lasted two months, and reports came to Manchester of weavers in the mills outside the town drilling, armed with sticks and staves. These drillings, say the weavers' principal poet and apologist, Samuel Bamford, in his minor classic *Passages in the Life of a Radical*, were peaceful, their intention being only to ensure orderly movement at meetings and "healthful exercise and enjoyment". The spinners' strike leader, an Irishman named John Doherty, was gaoled for his part in the affair. The 'masters', the cotton employers, went to every length to break the strike, refused to negotiate, misrepresented the workers' claims and generally left a rancour and sense of injustice among their employees which the passage of many years failed to eradicate.

In January 1819 one of the leading Radical reformers, Henry 'Orator' Hunt, spoke in St. Peter's Field. His theme was "annual Parliaments and universal suffrage", but he was abusive of authority, and before the meeting he attempted to harangue the members of the Exchange, who came to their newsroom window to watch him and his exultant followers carrying a flag inscribed "Hunt and Liberty" and a red staff surmounted by a red Cap of Liberty, the emblem of Reform. Other banners proclaimed "No Corn Laws".

A month later at Sandy Brow, Stockport, the special constables ill-advisedly tried to seize the Cap of Liberty at a Radical meeting and provoked disturbances rough enough to cause the Riot Act to be read three times. James Norris, the Manchester stipendiary magistrate, regretted the attempt to seize the Cap because "it gave the multitude an apparent triumph". The mob at Stockport was far more militant and aggressive than any that had yet assembled in Manchester, and Norris's fears of worse to come were justified. A few days after the Stockport incident verses were published which showed the feeling engendered.

> All hail! the day what I do see
> It is the Cap of Liberty,
> Placed on the Rights of Man:
> No Corn Laws! Britons shall be free!
> It is our Heavenly King's decree
> That man shall have his Liberty;
> And hinder it who can; . . .

Modern setting for modern art in the Whitworth

These bloated vampires rode about
Till one cursed hand was stretched out,
For th' Cap of Liberty;
Then vengeance tinged with bitter gall,
Burst from each heart both great and small,
And courage true was firm with all,
To drub the Cavalry.

Further meetings followed in June at Ashton-under-Lyne, Oldham, Bolton, Bury, Heywood, Manchester, Rochdale and other towns, again including Stockport, where on the 28th the two main speakers, a parson and the Radical baronet Sir Charles Wolseley, preached what in any context can only be designated as rebellion. No wonder that in mid-June Norris had forecast with astonishing accuracy to the Home Secretary, Lord Sidmouth, that "a very short period of two months at the longest is spoken of as the great Day of Trial . . . . a few weeks may blow this wicked conspiracy into a flame".

It is part of Left-wing dogma that Peterloo was an act of class war perpetrated by Lord Liverpool's government on the working-class, that the 60,000 people peaceably assembled in St. Peter's Field on 16th August 1819 to listen to Hunt's speech on reform were unprovokedly dispersed by the drunken cavalry who savagely sabred several innocent people to death and wounded many others, all on the orders of the panic-stricken specially-formed committee of magistrates. It has needed a Mancunian antiquarian bookseller of today, Mr. Robert Walmsley, to put the factual record straight 150 years after the event and after thirty years of patient and scrupulous research for his monumental book *Peterloo: The Case Re-opened*★.

The magistrates were alarmed about keeping order because an Act prohibiting large meetings or "seditious assemblies" had expired in 1818 after being in force just over a year. Sidmouth pointed out that they still had sufficient powers, and, although he understood their alarm and advised them to hold troops in readiness, he has been cleared by all the published historical documents of any instruction to put down meetings by force. In any case the magistrates had received expressions of concern from the inhabitants of several towns, one of which very reasonably

★ Manchester University Press, 1969.

said that "it is manifestly one thing to petition and remonstrate, and another thing to insult and menace". Might not the same thing have been said by the citizens of Belfast and Londonderry in 1969?

When the great Radical meeting in Manchester was called for 16th August it is hardly surprising that the authorities considered the possibility that it represented a flashpoint for revolution and that property in Manchester might be destroyed or damaged. The magistrates assembled at 11 a.m. at a house in Mount Street overlooking St. Peter's Field, and 100 yards from the hustings where Hunt was to speak. Troops were stationed in various parts of the town: the Manchester and Salford Yeomanry off Portland Street, regulars of the 15th Hussars and Cheshire Yeomanry in St. John Street, and other contingents of regulars in Lower Mosley Street, Brazennose Street and Dickinson Street. The crowds had begun to arrive at about 9 a.m., an astonishing sight, each contingent carrying banners and flags and Caps of Liberty. Bands were playing and slogans were shouted. The women and children were dressed in their best clothes, and there can be no doubt that for the vast majority of the 50,000 or 60,000 people this was a 'day out', peaceful and idealistic in its aims. But it is the bloody-minded handful who matter in these affairs. The scene has been brilliantly painted by Howard Spring in his splendid novel *Fame is the Spur*:

> There they were, then, those thousands upon thousands of Lancashire working folk, men, women and children, milling and shouting in the field that still stood open in the heart of the town. A holiday crowd for the most part, some of them intent, but not too seriously, on hearing what the speakers would have to say about this improbable question of their lives being made a little more bearable; and a few blackly set on a desperate venture. The bands brayed, the people shouted and cheered in front of the wagons from which they were to be addressed, and the hot August sun burned down. [In fact it was a dull, overcast day.]

Between the magistrates' house and the hustings (two farm carts tied together) was a double line of special constables. Hunt, who had been in Manchester for several days and had been behaving and speaking like the crude demagogue he really was, was due to speak at midday, but he was over an hour late and tempers began to fray in the meantime. The hustings were moved by the crush of the crowd and were surrounded by Hunt's supporters. When Hunt arrived a shout went up the like of which the 31-year-old chief magistrate William Hulton said he had never heard—"and I hope I never shall again". His opinion was that the town was "in great danger—the meeting did undoubtedly produce terror in the minds of the inhabitants".

Hunt had uttered seditious remarks at Smithfield, London, a few weeks earlier, and his conduct in Manchester had been anything but conducive to peaceful assembly. So Hulton decided to arrest him and his followers; but Nadin, the deputy constable, refused to serve the warrant without military aid because, as he said later, he and his men had been stoned in the New Cross district a few nights earlier when they had gone to remove some offensive posters. He knew the mood of the militants, and he probably knew that he was widely regarded as a coarse bully. Hulton wrote notes to the commanders of the various troops asking for their aid *to serve the Warrants* not to disperse the meeting. The Yeomanry, being nearest, arrived first. The Riot Act was read, but because of the noise no one heard it. At the hustings, as Robert Walmsley has proved beyond doubt—mainly by using Radical sources of information which have been over-looked—the militant Stockport section of the crowd attacked the Yeomanry. Hulton then said to the regular army commander: "Good God, sir, they are attacking the Yeomanry! Disperse the crowd."

The Hussars drew their swords, held them above their heads and moved into the crowd. In the mêlée, the crowd fled, some trying to unseat the riders and cut their girths. Against such actions the rider's only defence was to retaliate with his sabre. Most of the casualties were caused by panic, and several people were trampled to death by their fellows. No one knows the accurate casualty figure. Hunt always said that fourteen were killed and 648 wounded, but the truth seems to be nearer six dead (who included two of those on the side of authority) and about thirty hurt. It was certainly no massacre, as the term would usually be understood.

If the facts of Peterloo and the motives behind it are a good deal less lurid than Socialist propaganda has made out over the years—and George Saintsbury, writing eighty-two years before Mr. Walmsley, advised caution in the acceptance of Radical accounts

of the fiasco—there is no doubt that the incident inflamed public
opinion and played a part in bringing about the Reform Act of
1832. But why is Peterloo, a comparatively trivial affair not to be
compared with the riots in Bristol and Nottingham, still the
rallying-point in discussion of Reform? Why was Mr. Walmsley's
book so unwelcome to some shades of opinion? Why is Peterloo
so emotive a word still, causing heated debates in Manchester
City Council in 1969 when a proposal to re-name St. Peter's
Ward Peterloo Ward was (not for the first time) rejected?

The answer lies surely in the fact that this was the first and best
reported of British political gatherings outside London. *The
Times* sent a special reporter to 'cover' the meeting. He was on
the hustings and placed himself "in protective custody" when
Hunt was arrested, writing his famous report (which appeared on
19th August) in the New Bailey Prison, Salford. The Manchester
newspapers covered columns with their reports. It was an
inspired journalist on the staff of the *Manchester Observer*, who,
with Waterloo but four years in the past, coined the word
Peterloo and by that single idea alone probably ensured that the
incidents on St. Peter's Field would have a place in history far
beyond their merits or deserts. What's in a name, indeed!

To wish to see historical accuracy established and to wish to see
an event in its true context of the contemporary mood and
situation are often regarded as signs of reactionary political
sentiment. No one today is seriously going to say that the denial
to the British people of a franchise that we now regard as a
birthright was in any way defensible. Clearly there were oppression, tyranny and exploitation in the England of 1819. Yet it
is right that writers like Robert Walmsley should correct over-
emotional interpretations and sift fact from fantasy, lies from the
truth. Sam Bamford's graphic and moving description of Peterloo
is fine literature, but it "muddied the stream of history".

Archibald Prentice, a Manchester editor and author of the
much-quoted *Sketches and Recollections of Manchester* (1851), is
mercilessly discredited by Mr. Walmsley, but he ends his account
of Peterloo with an anecdote that must be true, because it is so
characteristic of genuine Lancashire humour. It concerns "poor
old Thomas Blimstone", who had been ridden over by the
Yeomanry. "I recollect him", Prentice writes, "standing in my
counting-house, with his two arms splintered up, and telling his

case to the relief committee. At the conclusion he said, 'And what is wur than aw, mesters, they'n broken my spectacles, and aw've ne'er yet been able to get a pair that suits me.' "

Peterloo was not the end of the story. The authorities remained nervous enough to prevent William Cobbett from entering Manchester on 30th November on his way to London from Liverpool after his visit to the United States; they had their fill of Radical orators in 1819. But two years later, as a contemporary newspaper recorded, "peace, cheerfulness and industry had returned to the town". The cotton trade was booming again, unemployment decreased and with it agitation. For the next four years all was well, and the manufacturers were helped by reductions in government taxation. In 1825 they promoted a Parliamentary Bill for the construction of a ship canal from Manchester to the Dee, a far-seeing project with an estimated expense of £1 million (10,000 shares of £100 each as capital), but the Bill was defeated and Manchester had to wait almost another seventy years for its Ship Canal.

Hard times returned in 1825–26. The good years had caused over-production and stockpiling: these stocks had to be sold off when world trade was again depressed before manufacture could begin again. So unemployment returned. Manchester put soup kitchens into operation for the needy, and £60,000 was raised in local and government aid for relief work among the distressed. The recently introduced paper currency was inflated and was a major cause of the national economic crisis, although in this respect the Manchester banks were solid enough to withstand the blizzard—but they refused notes from the dealers who came into the town from the country. The political temper of Manchester was now hardening into the liberalism of its great years, with an insistence on the need for international peace, a distrust of imperialistic tendencies and a growing resentment of England's constitutional limitations. The Chamber of Commerce condemned the paper currency and advocated the gold standard as a better means of protecting the workers' earnings.

But the hungry working-man of 1826 cared nothing for political and economic theorising. During March and April of that year loom-breaking on a big scale occurred in the outlying districts. In Manchester itself, in May, there was another mass meeting of unemployed after which a factory was burned down and food shops were plundered. Three years later the riots broke out on an even more savage scale, when the cotton unemployed were reinforced by silk workers from Macclesfield and Stockport, where a sudden slump in the silk trade had had disastrous effects. On 4th May 1829 Manchester virtually fell into the hands of the mob, who roamed the streets, attacking three factories and destroying their contents, burning another to the ground, looting shops and calling workers out on strike. The rioters pressed no political point: they were merely hungry and also angry with manufacturers and their machines. Eventually, without bloodshed, magistrates and dragoons restored order, but there must during those two or three days have been the seeds of a real, not a Peterloo, massacre in Manchester if more resistance had been offered or if the mob had been directed by a vicious-minded leader.

Although there were some disturbances in 1842 and 1848 during the Chartist agitations, worse at Ashton and Oldham than anywhere else, the riots of 1829 were the last serious outbreaks of violence in Manchester; and the passage of the Reform Bill in 1832 at last enfranchised Manchester and ended the ridiculous situation whereby country villages like Old Sarum and Newton-le-Willows returned two members to Parliament and one of the largest and most important industrial centres in Europe returned none.

The question inevitably arises: why, when there was so much injustice, oppression, squalor, hunger and poverty in the North-west of 1810–40 was there no equivalent of the French Revolution? Was it because the working-class was poorly organised and badly led? Was it because the 'masters' came from the working-class and not from the landed aristocracy—as one of Manchester's leading spinners, James Kennedy, said in 1828: "The only men who have made their fortunes have been those who started with nothing", in other words men of remarkable individual business sense and strength of will—or was it because the rise of poverty coincided with the rise of Methodism, and oppressed men preferred to sing hymns and Handel rather than to take arms against their sea of troubles? Or did they regard any violent protest as a doomed and hopeless way out, sure to be crushed by military force?

Something of all these, no doubt; but more important than any were some innate tolerance and wisdom in the Lancashire working man's nature. There is an example of this from Ashton-under-Lyne in 1848 in a letter written by some of the men at a local mill to the factory inspector complaining about the malpractices of the employers and ending:

> We give you our names as we are prepared to meet Mr.Whitaker before the Inspector. We wish him no evil. We bear him no grudge. But his father did not behave as he does. Nay, one of the oldest inhabitants, who remembers him very well, says the old man would turn in his grave if he knew how his sons were carrying on. Is it not a pity men should be so greedy and so rash when they have all this world can give?

The presence of men of that calibre in the ranks of the workers saved England from calamity. It explains how and why trade unionism developed in Lancashire as a peaceful means of giving the workers a voice against their employers, although the employers did not see it in that light. Manchester was notorious among the manufacturers of England as the 'hotbed' of working-class movements. As early as 1758 there had been a union of operatives, and in the 1790s there had been clubs of spinners and craftsmen. During the cotton strike of 1818 there had been an attempt to form a 'general union of trades', and one of the leaders of that attempt, John Doherty, in 1829 formed in the Isle of Man a 'grand general union of cotton spinners'. This was dissolved in 1831 when Doherty formed a national association for the protection of labour. This too was short-lived. A book called *Manchester As It Is* published in 1839 referred to trade unions as "common in Manchester" and added that " 'Strikes', as they are called, are by no means infrequent." The anonymous author of the book wrote:

> The frequent and insufferable annoyances which engineers have experienced from trades' unions—by which annoyances unionists are so absurd as to think that, ultimately, they can raise wages—have tended to give more force to that course of events which is destined to carry this country to the highest pitch of mechanical perfection.

During the 1850s numerous trades councils were formed, culminating in 1868 in the first Trades Union Congress, held in Manchester.

This chapter must end with an account of the political results of the foregoing and with a brief survey of the one and only time Manchester has been of considerable political significance, a period commemorated in the name of one of its most famous buildings, the Free Trade Hall.

Free Trade as a political doctrine was first propounded by London merchants in 1820—in this case the well-known saying "What Manchester thinks today, the rest of the country thinks tomorrow" did not apply. The idea that trade should be unrestricted and prices would find their own competitive levels was opposed by the Protectionist theory of a tariff duty on imported and foreign-made goods as a safeguard to British traders.

The outstanding and most hated feature of the tariff system was the Corn Laws, which were held in Lancashire to be responsible for the fluctuations (stop-go) in prosperity and the resulting social distress—this, at any rate, was how the manufacturers regarded it; their employees were less sure, and it was because of the workers' suspicion that Free Trade was a capitalist vested interest that the People's Charter, its adherents being called Chartists, gained its following. (The workers at this time, many of them illiterate, were easy prey for demagogues and could scarcely distinguish one 'cause' from another. At a Chartist meeting near Manchester in 1842 one speaker was heard to say that there was "a bit of a falling-out as to whether we're all to contend for the wage question or for the charter".)

An Anti-Corn Law Association was formed in London in 1836. In 1838 the 36-year-old M.P. for Wolverhampton, Charles Villiers, moved the first of several annual motions for an inquiry into the effects of the Corn Laws passed in 1828, which had precipitated hunger, strikes and trade recessions in many areas. The Manchester Anti-Corn Law Association was formed on 24th September 1838. Its two most powerful advocates were Richard Cobden, the calico printer who, though born in Sussex, had made his fortune in Manchester by the time he was 30, and John Bright, a cotton spinner and a Quaker, from Rochdale. In March 1839 the association and its local branches turned themselves into the Anti-Corn Law League dedicated to total repeal. The League put up candidates for the Commons. R. H. Greg of Styal was returned for Manchester later in 1839, Cobden for Stockport in 1841, and Bright for Durham in 1843.

The league achieved its end by anticipating modern methods of publicity—it made its views known by every means and in every way possible. It set up a headquarters in Market Street and thence poured pamphlets, books and handbills by the ton—100 tons alone in 1845, it was estimated. It raised money by bazaars and balls and subscription lists. Its speakers toured the country. It used the new penny post after 1840 to disseminate its literature. It was the first thoroughly organised propaganda movement in British history and it won. In 1846 Sir Robert Peel repealed the laws.

If ever there was an example of the acumen of business being put to political ends, it was the Anti-Corn Law League. The Manchester businessmen who had made fortunes lavished money upon it: it was never short of funds and, after its victory, there was £75,000 as an expression of gratitude to Cobden. Its first great meeting was held in the first Free Trade Hall, a wooden structure built on St. Peter's Field on a plot given by Cobden to house demonstrations by the League. About 4,000 people attended the opening banquet on 13th January 1840. Three years later a brick building replaced the wooden one and was opened on 30th January 1843, again with a league function.

On 31st January 1849, at a great banquet of the league, the announcement was made on the stroke of midnight, "Gentlemen, the Corn Laws are dead"—for final repeal had been delayed for financial reasons for three years after the passage of the repealing Act in 1846. And though it lingered on, the league was dead too, because its *raison d'être* had been removed.

Cobden and Bright were also associated with the political theory—it was hardly a movement—known as the Manchester School, and by the Germans as *Manchesterthum*. It sprang from the alteration in Manchester's political views already summarised, principally the belief that the way to true national power and international peace lay not through force of arms but through commerce and the arts, especially commerce. Cobden and Bright were in constant conflict with Lord Palmerston, who was not afraid of the idea of war as a solution to a knotty problem. Non-intervention was Cobden's creed, and he was the first to admit its general unpopularity at a time of dawning nationalism. The *Manchester Guardian* had by this time lost its radical way and supported Palmerston. It bitterly opposed Cobden and Bright, describing their 'school' as "the brood that have so long infested

Parliament". Bright's statue in Albert Square stares fixedly at the Town Hall with the expression of a man who could, if he would, tell much.

The 'school' broke up with Cobden's death, and its importance lay in its slow influence on political thought rather than in any special achievements. In its day its policy was regarded by opponents as wanting in patriotism; Cobden's remark that "all the Works of Thucydides were not worth one copy of *The Times*" was regarded as Mancunian Philistinism: only arts that made money were to be admired, were they?

Moreover the opposition of some of the 'school's' supporters to Lord Ashley's factory legislation (limiting hours of work and improving conditions for women and children) was regarded as confirmation of the hypocrisy of Cobden and Bright—they were cotton 'masters' and they defended their own interests, so it was said, under the guise of high-mindedness. As one writer said in 1848: "The Manchester bourgeoisie . . . is Liberal only so far as it believes Liberality, i.e. free trade, to be profitable." Nor did Bright's anti-clericalism endear him to the Victorian age, though we may chuckle today at his comment when Manchester's 'owd church' became a cathedral with a bishop: he regretted he hadn't been returned to Parliament in time to vote against this "calamity". Bishops, he said, had "never yet to his seeing done any good and had to his seeing done multitudinous evils".

Actually, Manchester's bishops, who have included William Temple, have not been a notably evil bunch. It was Temple who met a distinguished Manchester journalist as he was leaving the clergy's favourite club.

"Where are you going?" he asked, "I wanted a talk about cricket with you."

"I'm going to the dentist."

"Well, take my advice, my good fellow, and while you're there have 'em all out. The Almighty is a wonderful chap but with all His omniscience He never could make a decent set of teeth."

With the end of the Manchester School, Manchester's political influence devolved upon individuals rather than ideas. Gladstone and Disraeli made important speeches there, Winston Churchill and Arthur Balfour represented it in the Commons. Aneurin Bevan made his famous "vermin" speech in Belle Vue. C. P. Scott's influence upon and quarrels with Lloyd George are a part of Liberal history rather than Manchester's. Far more important than Peterloo in its consequences was the emergence of the middle-class radical voice which shaped English provincial life and led, ultimately, to the apotheosis of Liberalism, the 1906 Government. Yet how ironical it was that Scott, a personification of Manchester's liberal-radicalism, its voice in fact, should through his attachment to Lloyd George have helped to destroy the effective political power and importance of the party he and his paper supported. Scott's friendship with Lloyd George dated back to the Boer War, which they both opposed. "I have affinities with Ll. G. I am a realist," Scott wrote. "Perhaps I am flattered by the fact that he . . . constantly seeks my opinion and usually acts upon it. Perhaps I delude myself, and the wizard all the time is playing with me. I am an unsuspicious person, but somehow I don't think it's quite like that." No, Scott wasn't a humbug, as has been suggested; but it's a relief to realise that the High Priest of Radical Journalism had feet of clay, like the rest of us.

SIX

PRINCES' PALACES

"WHAT self-confidence those Manchester Victorians had!" One has often heard that said, and it is true enough. What gave them self-confidence? In a word, prosperity. The people who mattered in Manchester were wealthy. True, trade had its ups and downs. Plenty of small traders went bankrupt; but many more did not. Money breeds confidence. I don't suppose the Irish living in Fennel Street or the English living in Ancoats and Chorlton-on-Medlock were very confident, but they didn't count. No one consulted them about how Manchester should be run or how it should look. So we come back to the original thesis: Manchester was a confident city, and that confidence was expressed not only in investments but in bricks and mortar, in edifices 'built to last', to show future ages that all was well.

Not only was it a confident city, it was a progressive city. It wanted certain things done, and it had the money to do them. It wanted the Corn Laws repealed, and it raised enough money to launch a campaign that had them repealed. It wanted new and splendid buildings, so it went to the best young architects and asked them to build them. When I say 'it' I don't mean the corporation, I mean the real powers of the Victorian city, the merchants who kept it going. The editor of the magazine *The Builder* described Manchester between 1840 and 1860 as "a striking example of prevailing good taste". He added:

> It is greatly to the credit of the merchants of the town that they have had the judgment to use the services of architects, in buildings in which they are seldom applied to, and it is greatly to the credit of the architects that these appeals have been replied to by them almost universally in the best manner.

It was an architects' competitive paradise, and the Manchester architects kept it to themselves. This same editor of *The Builder*, reporting in 1852 on a visit to Manchester by the Liverpool Architectural Society, wrote: "They [the Manchester architects] showed not the slightest interest or the smallest amount of good feeling towards the visitors."

The Manchester men of the nineteenth century are often described as merchant princes. It is a good description, and in one respect particularly apposite. Princes work in palaces, and the merchant princes of the Industrial Revolution decided to work in them too. So it is that Manchester is uniquely rich in commercial palaces, the warehouses, built in the palazzo style and in the new materials of terracotta and iron. Of course they are, in a sense, deceptions, phoneys. They are not Italian palazzi, they are Manchester warehouses. But unless your sense of architectural propriety is so strong that you cannot stomach the idea of such a counterfeit, then you will probably, as I do, admire them for their magnificent solidity and grandeur, stationed through the city like a mighty architectural ostinato. The most famous of them is the S. & J. Watts Warehouse in Portland Street, built in 1851 by the firm of Travis and Mangnall. Constructed from Derbyshire stone, iron, timber and 27,000 square feet of glass it is the most grandiose building in the city, pretentious perhaps but on the most elaborate scale and, as Professor Cecil Stewart pointed out, its style is no longer Italian or Renaissance, it is steadfastly mid-Victorian.

Most of the other great warehouses were built earlier and designed by Edward Walters. The first of them, built when the architect was 31 in 1839, was commissioned by Cobden for 15, Mosley Street. But the best Walters warehouse is at the corner of Aytoun Street and Portland Street, facing Piccadilly. Here you can see all the fantastic elaboration and ornamentation characteristic of the style—the curved windows, rich in detail, the corners rusticated from top to bottom, everything ornate and opulent. Walters also designed the Queen's Hotel in Piccadilly, but his most famous building was the third Free Trade Hall, destined to be as famous as a concert-hall as a political assembly.

His design won a competition to replace the second hall on the Peterloo site in 1853 and was completed in 1856. Some authorities say it derives from the Basilica at Vicenza, others that it is based

on the Gran Guardia Vecchia at Verona, which Walters visited in
1837. At any rate it was the culmination of the palazzo style. Only
the façade stands today. The interior was destroyed by bombs in
1940 while the hall, ironically, was being used as a warehouse, and
the interior was re-designed by Leonard Howitt and re-opened in
November 1951. The hall is known chiefly as the home of the
Hallé Orchestra—the old hall was imposing but gaunt and
uncomfortable, although acoustically superior to its successor,
which is discreetly modern in style and décor; but the need to
keep within the framework of the old building has meant a good
deal of skimping of accommodation space for the public.

Much of Manchester's history has taken place within the walls
of the Free Trade Hall. They echoed to the very first of all
performances of Elgar's first symphony in December 1908, and to
the first English performances of Berlioz's *Damnation of Faust* and
Symphonie Fantastique, both conducted by Hallé. It was there that
a huge meeting of cotton workers in 1862 pledged themselves to
assist the North in the American Civil War, although the stoppage
of raw cotton imports from the South brought famine and
poverty to the whole of Lancashire—an act of "sublime Christian
heroism", Abraham Lincoln said. It was there that Dickens gave
readings, Gladstone, Disraeli and Bright often spoke, that the
young Lloyd George and the young Winston Churchill had their
political apprenticeship. It was there that women suffragists first
called attention to their campaign when they were carried from
the hall out into Peter Street after creating a disturbance because
they were dissatisfied with answers Churchill gave to their
questions. When, in 1947, forty years later, Churchill received the
freedom of Manchester, the casket was made of wood saved from
the wreck of the hall, which became Corporation property in
1920 when it was bought for £90,000.

In 1860 Walters built the Manchester and Salford Bank, Mosley
Street, (now Williams Deacon's), which is perhaps his finest
building and is still among the three best buildings in Manchester
today.

The Bank of England in King Street, designed by Charles
Robert Cockerell, architect of the Ashmolean at Oxford, is
among the last English buildings in the Greek classical style, which
in 1845, the date of this masterpiece, had already been superseded
by the palazzo craze. Another splendid palazzo example is the

bank at the corner of St. Ann's Square and St. Ann Street, designed by J. E. Gregan for Sir Benjamin Heywood. (It is now another Williams Deacon's.) This building effortlessly solves a major design problem: it contains a large stone block (the bank) and a small brick block of offices, linked by an archway. If you can see it without too many cars parked alongside you will see the point.

The palazzo and classical styles were succeeded by the Gothic Revival, whose principal architect, in both senses, was George Gilbert Scott, a man, as has wittily been said, "full of ideas, few of them his own". He designed St. Pancras Hotel, but curiously enough he left very little mark on Manchester. But at Worsley he left what many consider to be his finest church, St. Mark's (1844), which has a Burne-Jones window and some Flemish stained glass. Other Scott churches in the area are Christ Church, Denton, a poor example; and St. Paul's, New Cross, which is better.

The man whose name is for ever associated with the Gothic revival in Manchester was Alfred Waterhouse, born in 1830, a pupil of Richard Lane and a disciple of John Ruskin, whose advocacy of Venetian Gothic in *The Stones of Venice* (1851) he took to heart, and then some. At the age of 27 Waterhouse won a competition for Manchester Assize Courts against the rivalry of Thomas Allom, Norman Shaw, Cuthbert Broderick and Thomas Worthington. In this competition, incidentally, 940 drawings were submitted. The building was opened in 1859 and Ruskin loyally declared that the Great Hall was "the most truly magnificent Gothic apartment in Europe". Alas, we cannot judge the truth of this, for the courts were bombed in 1940 and only the judge's lodgings and the Great Ducie Street façade survive as impressive reminders of a glory that is gone. It was only natural and just that, having designed the assize courts, Waterhouse should have been asked to design the new gaol on the Strangeways site to the north-east. No one, least of all the inmates, would vote this as one of his best efforts.

Waterhouse was soon much in demand elsewhere than in Manchester. He was prolific, and his failures are as numerous as his successes. The Natural History Museum at Kensington is his. Hit or miss? Marginally the former. Misses are Pembroke College, Cambridge; the Metropole at Brighton; and the hideous Refuge building in Oxford Road, Manchester; and the

Theatre workshop in the university

near-by St. Mary's Hospital, Whitworth Street. No matter.
One glorious hit outweighed all the rest.

In 1866 Manchester launched a competition for a new town
hall—spurning the more pretentious city hall name—to replace
Goodwin's King Street building which was now too small. The
new hall was to be on a triangular site on the Town's Yard. There
were 130 entries, and these were whittled down to a short list of
eight. But the two assessors recommended Waterhouse's, which
they had placed fourth, because it was the cheapest, it provided
for natural ventilation and had more window-light. The city
council demanded a second report before they agreed to build the
Waterhouse design. In this way Manchester obtained the great
building that embodies its character in stone.

Today, now that the centre of Manchester is smokeless, the
Town Hall has been cleaned and can be seen as it was on the day
it opened, 13th September 1877. The foundation stone was laid
nearly ten years earlier, on 26th October 1868. To those of us who
grew up knowing the Town Hall—and many other buildings—
as almost completely black (and possessing in that condition a
certain robust extra magnificence), the soot and grime of nearly a
century eliminating many of the elaborate carvings which the
architects had optimistically devised, it was a revelation to see it
in its light stone dress. To appreciate its triangular shape it is best
to stand on the Princess Street-John Dalton Street side of Albert
Square. From this viewpoint one can see Waterhouse's masterly
use of space, with the huge central hall separated by courtyards
from the surrounding offices. The courtyards provide light for the
centre of the building and are approached from Cooper Street.
Their bridges, with coloured tiles and a mass of leaded glass, are
high romanticism.

The hall's exterior is impressive enough, particularly the Albert
Square front, a cadenza of decoration and detail and turrets and
carved figures, but the interior is breathtaking, with its groined
vaulted entrance, a huge vestibule and two marvellous staircases,
with open traceried screens. The reception rooms on the first floor
overlook Albert Square and make a dramatic setting for civic
functions. On the left at the top of the finer staircase is the Great
Hall, famous for its murals by Ford Madox Brown depicting
scenes from Manchester's history and equally remarkable for its
heraldic ceiling, where, sometimes bathetically placed, are the

Humphrey Chetham in his baronial hall

arms of Paris, Salford, Vienna, Genoa, Bolton, Tokyo, etc.

To obtain the full dramatic effect of the Town Hall, walk from the Midland Hotel up Mount Street. First there is the circular, neo-classical Central Library, then the neo-Gothic Town Hall Extension (1938) and, crowning all, the great tower of Waterhouse's hall. Though the styles are so different, they look right together. I realise, of course, that my enthusiasm for the Town Hall is not generally shared, though it is no longer quite so fashionable to detest it utterly or to regard it as a civic Gormenghast. Some madman, I believe, after the Second World War urged that it should be demolished. Quite apart from the enormous and unnecessary expense involved in providing a replacement, this would be an act of vandalism of the most barbaric kind. To replace Waterhouse's Town Hall in Manchester would be like an unsuccessful heart transplant, for this hall is the heart of the city. What is more, the Lord Mayor lives in it.

The twelve Madox Brown murals were completed after the hall was opened. Much to the artist's annoyance, the subjects were chosen by a council committee: he wanted to include Peterloo, but, as ever, this thorny subject set off political arguments and was excluded. (There is now a modern mural of it, not a very thrilling one, in the foyer of the Free Trade Hall.) The Madox Browns are, of course, a celebrated pre-Raphaelite treasury in a city which can boast several pre-Raphaelite treasures. A perpetual irritant to the historically-minded because of their inaccuracies and anachronisms, nevertheless the murals are visited by thousands of people every year, none of whom is likely to forget the depiction of John Dalton collecting marsh-gas, a sober warning of the terrors that can follow apparently harmless scholarly activity.

Waterhouse's last Manchester building was the university on Oxford Road, an essay in strangely conflicting styles, culminating in the Whitworth Hall frontage of oriel windows and lots of tracery. It has not yet been cleaned, but Manchester is fortunate that, unlike his Liverpool University building, Waterhouse did not build it in the red brick which he came to favour and which some architectural wit dubbed 'Slaughterhouse Gothic'.

Another great Victorian Manchester architect was Thomas Worthington, born in Salford. He too spent an impressionable youth in France and Italy and started to rebuild them in Manchester and district (a public baths in Stretford being designed 'in

Lombardic style', forsooth). His most famous work is passed every day by thousands of Mancunians, who give it perhaps a casual glance, if that. He won in 1862 the competition for a 'receptacle' to contain the statue in memory of Prince Albert which the mayor had commissioned. He devised a medieval shrine in the Florentine manner. By a strange coincidence, Scott's design for an Albert memorial in Kensington used the same idea fifteen months after Worthington's had been published. Sited in a recently cleared area to be known as Albert Square, the memorial must for a brief time have dominated its surroundings. Now it is dwarfed by the Town Hall. Worthington described Manchester as "the Florence of the nineteenth century". Certainly it could not have been laid at his door if the city had lacked Italian Gothic.

Most of the Victorian churches built around Manchester are monuments to an excessively sombre and doomsday approach to religious feeling. One exception is Bodley's St. Augustine, Pendlebury (1870), a fine example of French Gothic; and the other the Roman Catholic Church of the Holy Name, Oxford Road (1869), designed by J. A. Hansom, better known for the two-wheeled cab named after him in 1834. This, too, is French Gothic, a little out of place in this district, but a dramatic spectacle.

Manchester has another famous Roman Catholic church, built as early as 1794. This is St. Mary's, Mulberry Street, between Deansgate and Albert Square and best reached from Brazennose Street. St. Mary's is popularly known as the 'Hidden Gem', not because it is hard to find—though the name is apposite from that point of view also—but because Cardinal Vaughan, when he was Bishop of Salford, said of it "No matter on which side of the church you look, you behold a hidden gem." In fact the gem is less hidden these days, thanks to the good taste of the builders of a modern block on Brazennose Street who have left a wide through-way which gives a view of the church.

A period of leadership is often followed by a lean period and towards the end of the nineteenth century Manchester lost its architectural progressiveness. It became self-conscious, stylised and all too often ridiculous. Salomons' Reform Club in King Street of 1870 is a pointer towards decline, so was the deplorable warehouse built by F. H. Oldham in Blackfriars Street. The Midland Hotel, the Whitworth Art Gallery and the Municipal Technical School in Sackville Street and Whitworth Street, not to mention the Fire Station in London Road, were to win Manchester a reputation for ugliness that none of the better earlier buildings has been able to override. Whitworth Street as a whole, in fact, represents the final fling of Commercialism Rampant. Glazed brick and terracotta, it has none of the grandeur of Portland Street. It is a monument to the parvenu, and one can feel no kind of admiration for its drab warehouses.

Victorian Gothic had its last late flowering in Basil Champneys's John Rylands Library in Deansgate, designed in 1890 on a commission from Mrs. Enriqueta Rylands as a memorial to her husband, a self-made textile merchant, and to house one of the world's most important collections of medieval books and manuscripts. In red sandstone (recently cleaned from the all-pervading black) it is an elaborate combination of the Gothic Revival with art nouveau detail and trivia. I don't admire it very much but some do, and its contents are one of the city's glories. Its interior uses space in an admirably extravagant manner. Here, in the gloom and quiet of the vaulted Reading Room, are alcoves where students and scholars may read undistracted. Rare classics, maps, writings on skin, silk and stone, a manuscript by Petrarch, a 'Wicked Bible' enjoining us to commit adultery—these are but a few of the priceless books and manuscripts which make the John Rylands the object of pilgrimages by researchers from all over the world.

One thing—again it must be emphasised—is striking above all else about Manchester's nineteenth-century building activity. None of it was directed towards dwelling-houses. The conversion of Manchester into a workshop, a nine-to-five city, was complete. Up went the warehouses, the churches, the institutes, the mills, down came the old residential property; and the existing dwelling-areas became more crowded. The workers were left in their slums near the city; they could not afford to move further out until the trams came in the 1890s. But the better-off had gone years before, gone to Victoria Park, to Broughton and Eccles, to Fallowfield, Withington and Didsbury and, when the railways spread, to Altrincham, Bowdon and Hale, to Wilmslow and Alderley Edge, later still to Southport and North Wales. Gone so that their children could breathe cleaner air and so that they could escape that cloud of smoke, those dense fogs and the soot in the atmosphere.

Manchester at the turn of the century must have been at its
drabbest and blackest and noisiest. Photographs show how
workaday it looked, with its cobbled streets, its darkly dressed
inhabitants, its ugly tramcars. Today's Mancunians do not know
how lucky they are, with clean buildings staying clean, trees at
last in Albert Square—planted with admirable civic philanthropy
by the *Manchester Evening News* to mark its centenary—flowers in
Piccadilly and, as will be related later, the chance of impressive
new development, with people, not only the Lord Mayor,
sleeping in the city at night.

It cannot be said, however—or I cannot say, at any rate—that
they are specially lucky in the architecture of today. Glass and
concrete, rectangular and symmetrical, are like a uniform making
each English city the almost exact replica of its neighbour.
Perhaps one can work up a small amount of enthusiasm for Albert
Bridge House, even though it is largely inhabited by income tax
collectors, and for the CIS skyscraper, but they cannot compare
in line or character with the Victorian splendour which gives
Manchester its individuality and which should be jealously
preserved. Manchester's last really great buildings were Vincent
Harris's Central Library and Town Hall Extension. Indeed has any
modern architect faced a more formidable task than that of
grafting an extension on to Waterhouse's Town Hall? Yet
Harris's building succeeds superbly. It makes no effort to repeat
the unrepeatable or imitate the inimitable, but by its solid,
massive bulk, its spare lines, its sense of scale it becomes the exact
counterpoint of Waterhouse's main theme; and the curved walk
between the Library and the Extension is a wonderfully exciting
piece of townscape with a touch of ominous mystery that keeps
its thrill from becoming too familiar. Harris perhaps owed much
to the example of Lutyens, whose Portland stone Midland Bank
in King Street outfaces the Reform Club, but he surely achieved
his own immortality in his splendid seizing of a grand opportunity
to give Manchester a twentieth-century focal equivalent of the
triumphs of half a century earlier. The finest artistic addition to
Manchester since the Second World War is not a building but the
stained-glass screen memorial in the airport concourse to the
60,000 airborne men trained at Ringway. A mosaic of colours
depicting the fields as seen from the air it is, though poorly sited,
moving and imaginative art, a striking contrast to the incon-

gruous huge Venetian glass chandeliers which hang in the concourse.

There remains one further Victorian achievement to chronicle, not a building but architectural in its way: the Ship Canal, perhaps the most important and imaginative project in Manchester's history. It arose from hard times. From 1872 until 1896 was a bad time for trade, on the whole—is it just coincidence that the 'confident' architecture of prosperity was replaced by the cheap and nasty of the post-1870 depression era? To maintain its livelihood Manchester's business community had to ensure cheap and quick transport of its products out of Lancashire and equally quick and cheap import of raw materials. The railway companies' goods charges soared. The old idea of a ship canal was revived in 1882 by the engineer Daniel Adamson at a meeting in his Didsbury house 'The Towers', a typically Mancunian Gothic pile which is now the Shirley Institute, headquarters of the cotton industry's research organisation, and was sometimes known as the Calendar House because it has twelve towers, fifty-two rooms and 365 windows. The canal was at once opposed by Liverpool, by the railways and by some Manchester merchants with interests in the Liverpool shipping lines.

Adamson and his friends, the first Ship Canal Committee, decided to pilot a Bill through the House of Commons. It took them three years and cost them £350,000. The Lords and the Commons rejected it in turn. Committee stage was protracted beyond all that seems necessary, the Lords calling 151 witnesses. But Adamson refused to be discouraged and when, in 1885, the Bill was passed through both Houses he was greeted by Manchester like a conquering hero: banquets, processions, triumphs. There was still much to accomplish, however, raising the capital being the prime delay. Work on cutting the canal began in 1887; in 1890 Adamson died; the contractor died, too, and a new contract had to be negotiated. Money ran out, but in 1891 Manchester Corporation lent £5 million towards the final cost of £14 million (double the original estimate) and gained majority representation on the Board of the Company. On 1st January 1894 the 36-mile canal was opened to shipping, in time to take advantage of the trade recovery which lasted until 1914 and made Manchester, as an inland port, one of the busiest in the country. On 21st May 1894 Queen Victoria

officially opened it and knighted the city's Lord Mayor, Anthony
Marshall.

Construction of this great waterway presented many problems.
It involved lifting five railways, including the main line from
London, 75 feet above canal level. The tidal River Gowy was
diverted under the bed of the canal. Manchester is 60 feet above
sea level, so the canal was divided into five sections by locks which
'lifted' the water 13 to 16 feet at a time. At the sea entrance, locks
keep the water in when the tide ebbs. The most notable engineering feat is the Barton Aqueduct. There had been an aqueduct at
Barton, near Eccles, since Brindley built the Bridgewater Canal
in 1761 and took it over the Irwell. The lower course of the Irwell
became part of the Ship Canal, so Brindley's aqueduct was
replaced by an aqueduct and a road bridge. Whenever a ship
passes up or down the canal at this point, the aqueduct swings,
gates at either end imprisoning the water of the Bridgewater
Canal. At the same time the adjacent road bridge swings aside.

In its first year of operation the Ship Canal handled 925,000
tons of cargo. Today the figure is getting on for twenty times that
amount. Today the huge cargo ships of Manchester Liners can be
seen picturesquely gliding through the green fields of Cheshire on
their way to the sea. The port has invested heavily in roll-on,
roll-off facilities and container-ships for a transatlantic ice-
breaking service.

The canal is a genuine lifeline which, after the decline of cotton,
has kept the engineering and distributive trades of Manchester in
good business not only on the Trafford Park estate but throughout
the region. But it lately faced a new threat. The Manchester Ship
Canal Company was among the authorities due to be taken over
by the proposed National Ports Authority until the Conservative Government redeems its pledge to repeal the Labour
Government's legislation. With profits in 1969–70 of over £1
million, the Board of the Ship Canal Company felt entitled to
declare strong views on nationalisation. In the words of its
chairman, Sir Leslie Roberts:

> We do not see that what is proposed in the Ports Bill will in any
> way enable a strong and progressive port industry to be established.
> We are convinced that real competition is vital if any industry is to
> be successfully run. We *have* been successful and our success can be
> attributed to independence of thought and action.

Manchester's businessmen, as represented by the Chamber of Commerce, were equally unconvinced that political change of this nature would lead to any advantages. "There are no grounds for the assumption", they said, "that central direction can be better than the existing experienced local direction."

It is just one more example of Manchester's transition period. "Change and decay in all around I see." But the sturdy Mancunian spirit remains phlegmatic about it all. During the lunch interval at Old Trafford not long ago I overheard a discussion by a group of men, average age 55, about the potential marvels of science. One of them was dubious. "Now come on, 'Arry," said the upholder of Progress, "you've got to face it. We live in a technological age." Harry's reply embodied generations of Lancashire wit and wisdom. "Give over," he said.

SEVEN

WHAT PRICE THE ARTS?

DINE in 1970 in Didsbury or Bowdon, or even Sale, and it's probable that before the evening is over the conversation will turn to the significance of provincial life today, obviously with special application to Manchester. The rôle of Manchester concerns many people deeply and seriously: is it a city in decline, or dormant, or a city of destiny, a destiny not yet revealed but one firmly to be believed in, which will dawn with the completion of the vast university precinct? So the optimist among the diners may argue. Another is sure to say that with the decline of cotton and Liberalism, Manchester declined—when Cottonopolis became just Manchester again. And yet another may well chip in that the trouble with Manchester today is just this very conversation: Manchester has become too self-conscious, too introspective. It worries about its 'image', it apologises for its commercial past, even its weather—which is no worse than anywhere else's and often much better; it wants to be ultra-respectable, it even feels embarrassed to claim to be the second city in the kingdom as Cobden said it was and as indeed it still is.

Part of the trouble with the provinces is that the comparison is always with London; and it is a false, unfair comparison. London is bound to win: it has been there a long time, it is very big, it is, or was, well planned, it is the capital city, the seat of government, the home of royalty and pageantry, the centre of a widespread and multifarious cultural life. It has 9 million inhabitants and a constant 'floating' population of visitors and tourists. No provincial city can compete to equal all this, and if it is wise it won't try. But it can provide something different.

It is also misleading to compare the Manchester of today with bygone Manchester. Apart from the obvious danger of rose-coloured spectacles of memory, comparisons with the past usually and conveniently ignore the changed context of the times. It is easy to produce figures of the number of theatres, of debating societies, of art galleries in Manchester of, say, the 1930s and produce the figures for 1969 and say, "That proves it, the place is dying." Such a superficial comparison ignores the different social life of today, the much wider choice of leisure activities: television, superb gramophones, radio—all in your home—cars to take you much further much quicker: a trip to Stratford-upon-Avon, for example, is not very difficult to manage as an evening out. And the fast train or the plane or the motorways lead to London, with its multiplicity of cultural activities.

This changed social outlook—always remembering, too, that the numbers interested in theatres and concerts are a minority, albeit a growing one—is responsible as much as anything for the altered pattern of cultural life in Manchester. Not that it is a good thing for people in Manchester to say we don't need plays or opera here, we can easily go to Drury Lane or Covent Garden and get them when we want. To rely on another city to provide the nourishment of the arts is a swift and sure way to moribundity and to turn Manchester into an empty shell, smokeless, clean, well-planned, maybe, but lifeless. In any case, not everyone can afford to make these journeys.

What Manchester, what any provincial city, must do as it approaches the twenty-first century is to decide what it wants culturally: to rely on touring companies, on second-hand arts; or to develop something of its own, a theatre with a particular standard and outlook that London cannot rival, an opera company that combines an enterprising policy with a policy of mixing distinguished guest artists with the up-and-coming? No one can give glib or easy answers, especially as the economic circumstances of the day are all-important. But it seems to be unquestionable that a city must provide its own artistic life as automatically as it provides its drains if it is to be a worthwhile place in which to live. As Loraine Conran, the director of the City Art Gallery, said when criticised for spending a six-figure sum on a Stubbs, "to persuade the right kind of people to come to live here you need other things besides an ambitious slum-clearance programme".

If the increasing hours of leisure cannot be filled satisfyingly and with variety and width of choice, it will be a major failure at the door of educationists and of municipal authorities. Whatever the problems, whatever the expense, whatever the conflicting interests, somehow this must be done. It is surely no accident that the most famous Manchester artistic organisation, namely the Hallé Orchestra, developed in Manchester, set its own standards, its own tradition and was sustained through lean times and good times by the support of the people of Manchester.

Manchester means different things to different people. To some, it is the apotheosis of ugliness, and no amount of change will move them from that unyielding opinion. To some it is a city where everyone loves music, or is serious-minded about serious subjects, a city of democrats and radical idealists. But to many more it is still the city described by an American businessman who visited it in 1825:

> The whole community seems to be absorbed in business. The citizens of Manchester, taking them collectively, are not very polished or very hospitable. They are in general uncourteous to strangers. Money seems to be their idol, the god they adore, and in worshipping their deity they devote but a small portion of their time to those liberal pursuits which expand the mind.

Being inhospitable is a charge that would hardly be brought against Mancunians today, but the implied charge of Philistinism is often repeated. Did all work and no play make Jack of Manchester a dull boy? It's easy, of course, to see how and why the arts were left behind or left to a few in Manchester. The place developed rapidly and ungovernedly. The men who gave Manchester its wealth and therefore became wealthy themselves were self-made men, men who had had nothing, especially education, except for the ability to work, to see one jump ahead in business, to concentrate ruthlessly on developing a canny instinct for knowing how to make money earn more money; men in the pattern of the barber Richard Arkwright, whose inventions had earned him fame, wealth, a knighthood and ideas of opulence that took him on one occasion to Derby "accompanied by a number of gentlemen etc on horseback, his javelin men 30 in number, exclusive of bailiffs, dressed in the richest liveries ever seen there".

To most of these men, the idea of spending their money on buying a picture, or supporting the theatre or the concert-hall was not only alien, it would never have occurred. As G. M. Trevelyan has written, "neither machine industry nor evangelical religion had any use for art or beauty, which were despised as effeminate by the makers of the great factory towns of the North". So from the very beginning of the nineteenth century there was a division in Manchester life between the men of business, the *nouveau riche* of the lower classes, and the intellectuals who joined the Literary and Philosophical Society and founded the Statistical Society and the Royal Manchester Institution. The division became really serious and long-term in its effects when the town council was formed and most of its places were filled by the men of business rather than by those with higher than commercial aims and outlooks.

It is from this tragic division that Manchester found itself on one classic occasion with a Lord Mayor who commended the Art Gallery to a distinguished visitor in these terms: "None of your manufactured stuff, lad. Real masterpieces in there, all 'and-painted." C. P. Scott, at the opening of the City Art Gallery in the summer of 1883, noted in a letter to his wife how, at the civic dinner in the evening, the distinguished artistic guests "were all placed *any* where", and Holman Hunt was seated next to an Alderman who scribbled a note to his opposite neighbour asking "Who or what is Mr. Holman Hunt?" I have myself been in the company of Sir John Barbirolli when, in the interval of a Hallé concert during the 1950s, he was asked by the Lord Mayor, "What orchestra is it here tonight?"

These are perhaps unfair examples which concern individuals rather than general attitudes. After the mid-1840s the edge was taken off the initial philistinism and the town began to burgeon. Wealthy men poured money into the place and splendid institutions began to function. But it was on the humanities rather than the arts that this beneficence showered—on providing better education, better apprenticeships, on smoke abatement, on public parks, on public libraries, on medical research, on social service, on housing.

When C. P. Scott first went to Manchester in 1871 he threw himself and some of his money into improving conditions of housing among the poor, telling his father "it may be that the squalor of our great cities can only be remedied by the action of the State or the municipality, but at least it is well that, as in the case of education, individual effort should first break up the ground". There, in a sentence, is what made Manchester great—individual effort. But the delay in supplementing that effort in certain fields was often, if not fatal, at the least drastically injurious. (Over thirty years later, incidentally, one of Scott's sons went to live and work in Ancoats and died from tuberculosis contracted there.)

Manchester in the mid-nineteenth century was fortunate in its benefactors and in the men who went to live there. Its university grew from the bequest of a cotton spinner, John Owens, who left £96,000 for the foundation of a college for instruction to be given "in learning and science". So in 1851 Owens College opened at 21, Quay Street, in a house once lived in by Cobden (it is now the County Court almost opposite the Opera House), but was a failure, having only thirty-three students five years later. During the 1860s, despite the cotton famine caused by the American Civil War which brought poverty and distress on a devastating scale to Lancashire, Manchester men raised a quarter of a million pounds to make the college into a foundation worthy of the city. Famous Manchester names took a leading part in this campaign, some of them of German origin, others thoroughbred Lancastrians, Ashton, Barlow, Worthington, Taylor, Armitage, Falkner, Donner and Behrens. In 1873 the college moved to the new Waterhouse buildings in Oxford Road, in 1880 it became the first constituent college of the Victoria University (the other two being Leeds and Liverpool) and in 1903 it became independent. It brought to Manchester scholars like Henry Roscoe, Samuel Jevons, T. F. Tout, Samuel Alexander—great philosopher who became an O.M.—and Adolphus Ward. In the young editor of the *Manchester Guardian* these men found comparable intellect and vision. The bishop from 1870 was James Fraser, another man of humanitarian sympathies in advance of his day who once arbitrated in a strike. Then there were industrialists of the generosity and mental stature of Sir William Mather and Sir Thomas Fairbairn.

That none of these men gave the city a magnificent theatre or an opera house is scarcely to be wondered at, though it might be regretted. There was, after all, a Non-conformist spirit in the

North-west that regarded such things as theatre-going as the work of the devil. In any case, these were the pleasures of the comparative few and the Victorians' concern in Manchester was for the betterment of the many. They put plumbing and sewers before Shakespeare and Donizetti. Also, the theatre already existed, Manchester had its concerts, opera could be heard there pretty often—these things did not count among the priorities. But it must not be thought that Manchester was oblivious of the need for artistic beauty, and it proved it with the 1857 exhibition.

In 1845 Manchester had staged an exhibition of industrial products, a pioneering effort in this line that has been completely overshadowed in history by the Great Exhibition in Hyde Park in 1851 in Paxton's Crystal Palace. Since London had stolen Manchester's exhibition idea, Manchester now determined to steal the crystal palace idea, and in 1852 a committee was formed to build a crystal palace as the home for a vast collection of art treasures. Thirty-two Manchester businessmen gave £1,000 each towards the exhibition and sixty gave £500 each. Imagine the results if commerce gave the 1970 equivalent of £62,000 to the arts.

The exhibition site was at Old Trafford, roughly where the White City is today, sensibly attached to the new railway station there so that visitors could go straight into the exhibition hall. An enormous building went up, 656 feet long, 200 feet wide. The sides were made of corrugated iron and the roof was a semi-circular span of 104 feet, the central part being glazed. Inside this building was gathered the largest single exhibition of artistic treasures that the world had known, a remarkable feat of organisation because most of the famous pictures were then in private collections. Despite the attitude of one duke who asked "What do you want with art in Manchester? Keep to your cotton-spinning," such pictures as Gainsborough's "Blue Boy"; the Rokeby Venus; Van Dyck's "Charles I", lent by Queen Victoria; a large number of Turners; water-colours by David Cox, P. de Wint and Girtin; examples of Murillo, Hobbema, Titian, Rembrandt, Velasquez, Rubens and Veronese, Landseer, of course, and Millais's "Autumn Leaves", now a treasured part of the city's permanent collection, could be seen; also statues galore, furniture, Dresden china, Wedgwood, Sèvres, and examples of the goldsmith's art. Something like 12,000 exhibits in all. The public's favourites were Wallis's "Death of Chatterton"—there was always a crowd round it—and a picture of some fruit in which the strawberries looked so invitingly real that children were led away from it howling with frustration.

It was a fine summer in Manchester in 1857 and after the exhibition was opened by Prince Albert on 5th May it was visited by 1,335,915 people before it closed on 17th October. Receipts were £98,000 against expenditure of £99,000, but the sale of the building materials offset the loss. Visitors came from all over England to see the pictures. Mrs. Gaskell, at her house in Plymouth Grove—a rural district then—wrote that her home was "fuller than full, day and night" during the summer. One great permanent institution sprang from the exhibition, the Hallé.

Manchester's musical tradition did not begin with Hallé. Mention has already been made of the subscription concerts attended by the leisured class, and perhaps by Prince Charles Edward, in the 1740s. Thirty years later a weekly meeting of flautists in a tavern was the beginning of the Gentlemen's Concerts, which flourished enough to merit the building of a hall in Fountain Street in 1777, the year in which the first three-day musical festival was held in the town, organised by Sir Thomas Egerton. The Gentlemen's Concerts were twelve in a season, six miscellaneous and six choral. At the public concerts, evening dress was obligatory; paradoxically the 'private' concerts were less formal. Handel, Mozart, Haydn and Corelli were the most favoured composers.

In 1831 a new hall was built in Lower Mosley Street, where the Midland Hotel is now. By 1839 the concerts had 600 subscribers at five guineas each, each member being entitled to three tickets. There was usually a waiting list of 200 names for membership. The orchestra was about fifty in strength. Although Mendelssohn conducted *Elijah* in Manchester in 1847, its musical standards were in decline at this date, and in 1848 one of the directors of the Gentlemen's Concerts, a calico printer named Hermann Leo, learned that the 29-year-old pianist Charles Hallé, whom he had heard in Paris, had been driven to exile in London by the Revolution in France. Leo wrote to Hallé, telling him that Manchester was "ripe to be taken in hand" by someone who would "stir the dormant taste for the art" of music. Although he had had a similar offer from Bath, Hallé agreed to give Manchester a trial. There is no statue or memorial in Manchester to Hermann Leo, but there ought to be. He persuaded this remarkable young man, who for ten years had been part of a dazzling artistic circle in Paris, friend of Berlioz, Liszt, Wagner, Lamartine, Chopin, Garcia, Ingres, de Musset, Auber and Heine, among others, to settle in an ugly, dirty, industrial English city. Hallé's first impressions were unfavourable. He attended the recital given by his dying friend Chopin and was horrified to find how unimpressed the Mancunians were.

He played Beethoven's fifth concerto at a Gentlemen's Concert in September 1848 and wrote a vivid account of the occasion:

> The orchestra, oh, the orchestra! I was fresh from the Concerts du Conservatoire, from Hector Berlioz's orchestra, and I seriously thought of packing up and leaving Manchester so that I might not have to endure a second of these wretched performances. But when I hinted at this, my friends gave me to understand that I was expected to change all this—to accomplish a revolution in fact.

And change it he did. In 1850 he was appointed conductor of the Gentlemen's Concerts and made a clean sweep of the orchestra, appointing new players, insisting on more rehearsals, and insisting too on the concerts reaching a wider audience.

For the 1857 exhibition the committee enterprisingly invited Hallé to enlarge the Gentlemen's Concerts orchestra and to provide daily concerts. They gave him £4,515 with which to do it and he brought players from the Continent. When the exhibition closed Hallé reflected how wasteful it was to let this orchestra disperse. He decided, "at my own risk and peril", to engage the whole orchestra to give a series of weekly concerts. Thus on 30th January 1858 the Hallé Concerts began in the Free Trade Hall on a wet Saturday evening and have continued unbroken ever since. On his first season of thirty concerts he made a profit of 2s. 6d. After eight seasons the profit was over £2,000.

For the next thirty-seven years Hallé conducted the concerts, gradually raising the level of the programmes and inviting the world's great artists to appear with him. From the beginning he provided shilling seats for the less well-off, for he always regarded his mission as bringing beauty into the lives of people who were surrounded by ugliness. He kept his contacts with the great musicians on the Continent, but he grew to love Manchester.

For most of his time he lived in Greenheys which he saw in his

Monastic calm for scholars in John Rylands Library

lifetime change from a fashionable rural suburb to a smelly built-up area known locally as Frankfurt-on-Odour, a pun on the smell and the number of Germans who lived in the district. But when he first came he found a house in Victoria Park which his first wife described as "charming ... surrounded by delicious gardens ... and with all the comforts of an English habitation, carpets everywhere &c &c. ... Life is much cheaper than in Paris." When Hallé died in 1895 he had also given his adopted city a college of music, of which he was the first principal; and his funeral procession, with the crowds standing silent across the whole of the city from the Church of the Holy Name to Weaste Cemetery, Salford, had not been equalled since that of John Dalton in 1844, and was not to be equalled again until thirty-seven years later when C. P. Scott died.

His concerts were his private property and might have died with him had it not been for the public spirit of three business-men, Henry Simon, the industrialist, Gustav Behrens, the shipper, and James Forsyth, owner of a music shop, who guaranteed the concerts until a society was formed to run them on a non-profit-making basis. The orchestra was automatically known as the Hallé Orchestra, or affectionately as the 'Allé Band', an eloquent tribute to its delightful and beloved founder. Only one other orchestra of comparable standard—the Lamoureux—has as its title the name of its founder rather than of its city of origin. From that day onwards 'Hallé' meant Manchester, in musical terms.

From 1899–1911 the orchestra was conducted by Hans Richter, the outstanding conductor of his day, friend of Wagner, con-ductor of the first Bayreuth *Ring*, conduct of the Vienna Opera. He lived in Bowdon, not far from Adolph Brodsky, the great Russian violinist, who had also settled in the city as Hallé's successor at the college. Manchester's music was therefore cosmopolitan and able to attract the finest names in the world. Busoni, Petri, Backhaus, Richard Strauss, Elgar and Bartók were all associated with Edwardian musical Manchester. A glittering retrospect, but let it be remembered that on the December day in 1908 when Elgar's First Symphony was given its first performance by Richter and the Hallé, music that superficially might seem to represent the noonday splendour of British supremacy and wealth, the newspaper headlines in the city told of the terrible distress

On the Ship Canal

Engineering marvel, the Barton Aqueduct

because of yet another cotton slump, with two-thirds of the city
designated a slum area.

The *Guardian*'s critics included Ernest Newman, who savaged
Richter; and Samuel Langford, a great writer and a remarkable
personality, a nurseryman by trade, earthy of speech as of
profession, who would attend the concerts with the soil of his
garden clinging to his boots and remnants of his last meal perhaps
clinging to his waistcoat. Yet he wrote prose of the utmost sensi-
tivity and perception. He was incapable of small talk, and some
of his colleagues were often embarrassed to be with him on a
tram lest he might regale them with, for instance, obscenities
from an eighteenth-century libretto. Seeking a way to prevent
such a discourse, the author and dramatic critic C. E. Montague
once asked him: "How's Mrs. Langford?" This stopped Sammy
in his tracks and he thought for a long time, past two tram stops.
Then: "She's a little peevish today."

After the 1914–18 war, when the concerts were kept going
principally by Sir Thomas Beecham, another great character was
appointed conductor, the Ulsterman Hamilton Harty. Under his
brilliant and quixotic leadership the orchestra achieved new
triumphs until his sudden departure in 1933. For the next ten
years the orchestra had a chequered history until the society's
buccaneering and visionary chairman Philip Godlee invited John
Barbirolli to return from New York and to put the orchestra on
a more ambitious basis than it had previously experienced—over
250 concerts a year all over Britain, foreign tours, broadcasts and
recordings. What Barbirolli achieved is well known. He was like
the refiner's fire. Like Hallé, he grew to enjoy Manchester.
Instead of staying a year or two, as might have been expected, he
stayed for over twenty-five years as conductor-in-chief and then
was given the unique title of 'conductor laureate for life', because
neither he nor the Hallé committee nor the Manchester audience
could ever contemplate a time when J.B. was not associated with
the orchestra he had made his own. A tiny, frail figure, he was
nevertheless in every way but physically a big man, irreplaceable
as a personality who drew the crowds, a musician of exceptional
versatility and intensity. How many owe their love of music to
the work he did in the North can never be calculated.

Of course Manchester's loyalty to the Hallé often embarrasses
visiting orchestras, who find a small audience at their concerts—

not always, but often. But loyalty is not yet a crime, and the Hallé needed it during its financial struggles and crises during Barbirolli's time. He and Godlee fought for municipal support and slowly won it from a reluctant corporation who for years lagged thousands of pounds a year behind other cities, notably Liverpool, in support of an orchestra. To spend money on the Hallé, one councillor said, was "a disgusting waste of public money". Gradually, however, that kind of philistinism has diminished, and the attitude of the city council towards the orchestra today is one of proud patronage by a large majority vote.

This is not the place to write the history of the Hallé. Like the cotton trade, it has had its depressions and its halcyon days. (Rather like *Punch*, in some people's opinions it is never as good as it was.) Unlike the cotton trade, it has remained a premier feature of Lancashire life. No one can doubt that there will be thin times in the future, nor that they will be overcome, just as Hallé, Richter, Harty and Barbirolli overcame them. The orchestra's tradition is not a cliché, it is a living thing. There is a warmth, a personality, about the Hallé that immediately impresses visiting conductors. It has Lancashire humour and character, exemplified by two stories.

For fifty years its harpist was Charles Collier, a follower of Bacchus and also a devotee of cricket because the bar at Old Trafford was open throughout the day's play. He returned to rehearsal one day earlier than expected. "Did Lancashire win?" asked Barbirolli. "No," said Charles, "bad light closed the bar." Then there was Herbert Mitton, the bassoonist. In 1944 the Hallé was making one of its first Barbirolli recordings, possibly of Bax's third symphony. A telegram was brought into the Houldsworth Hall for Bert Mitton. He read it, folded it, said nothing, put it in his pocket and the recording went on. Afterwards Barbirolli learned that the telegram informed Mitton of his son's death in action.

But if music is on the whole in a healthy condition in Manchester today, what can be said of the theatre? Here, there is no doubt, the glory has departed. During the nineteenth century the town had a reputation for discriminating and adventurous theatrical taste. (It is amusing to reflect that it owed its first, wooden, Blackfriars Bridge over the Irwell to a theatrical

company who, in 1761, were performing in Salford and wished
to provide better and quicker access for their Manchester patrons.
They named it as a joke because the London Blackfriars Bridge
was being built at the time.) In the 1840s there were three theatres
in Manchester: the Theatre Royal, which had been destroyed by
fire in May 1844 on its Fountain Street site and rebuilt on its
present Peter Street site by September of the following year; the
'Queen's' (formerly the 'Minor') in Spring Gardens; and the 'City'
in Mount Street. John Knowles ran the Theatre Royal from 1842,
and it was his company which, in 1860, Henry Irving joined and
was surprised to find that both audience and critics were "more
discriminating and consequently more severe" than any he had
yet encountered. (The Hallé audience was also for long known as
one that was hard to please.)

Standards seemed to have fallen by the 1870s when Bishop
Fraser attacked the poor quality of plays and urged a more serious
approach. C. P. Scott had been depressed, on arrival at the
Guardian in 1871, by the dramatic criticism and even thought of
writing it himself. Later he helped to revive the standard by
providing critics who applied the highest yardstick to what they
saw, the first being A. W. Ward, later to be Principal of Owens
College; and others W. T. Arnold, Allan Monkhouse, Oliver
Elton and C. E. Montague, and, a little later still, James Agate. So
between 1880 and 1914 Manchester enjoyed a theatrical heyday.
In the nineties, for instance, French drama was regularly supplied
by Sarah Bernhardt, Coquelin and Modjeska. Bernard Shaw,
writing in the *Saturday Review* of 12th February 1898, mentions a
scheme (stillborn, as it turned out) in which Manchester was
"about to lead the way" to an "endowed [subsidised] theatre".
He attributed Manchester's fame in the arts to vanity, "the most
constant symptom of a shameful life", the founders of the city's
prosperity having amassed their fortunes "by the diligent exercise
of their moral deficiencies". The artistic institutions which existed
in London only, in Shaw's view, as "accidents of the fashion,
wealth and cosmopolitanism of the capital" were founded in
Manchester "by design". "It was worth a manager's while", he
pointed out,

> to produce, and produce superbly, such works as Byron's *Sardana-*
> *palus* in Manchester whilst the West End of London declared that
> even Shakespeare spelt ruin. . . . Manchester, too, has had of late

years its Independent Theatre and its experiments in Ibsen. And now it appears that to such notorious plotters for an endowed theatre as Judge Parry and Mr. Charles Hughes, the Lord Mayor of Manchester has said, "Will you walk into my parlour?".

But not for long.

What to most people represents the peak of theatrical achievement in Manchester was the comparatively brief period in the Edwardian age when the tea heiress Miss Horniman established in the city the first repertory theatre in England, she having just become disillusioned by her experiences as financial sponsor of the Abbey Theatre, Dublin. She started her company in the Gentlemen's Concert Hall in the Midland Hotel (a clause in the contract for the Midland site stipulated that it must provide a home for the concerts, whose hall had been pulled down to make way for the hotel) and later moved to the Gaiety Theatre, Peter Street, built by the architect Alfred Darbyshire in 1884 as the 'Comedy'. He was a friend of Irving and also gave Manchester the Palace Theatre.

With players of the calibre of Sybil Thorndike and Lewis Casson, Miss Horniman presented plays by Shaw, Granville Barker, Galsworthy and John Drinkwater. She also encouraged the 'Manchester School' of realistic contemporary drama—the 'kitchen sink' of its day, every bit as strong in its impact as Osborne's *Look Back in Anger* was fifty years later. Such plays as Allan Monkhouse's *An Englishman's Castle* and Harold Brighouse's *Hobson's Choice* were first acted by Miss Horniman's company. At this date (1908) there were eighteen other theatres in Manchester, and even then thirty cinemas. A company like the Independent Theatre Company, mentioned by Shaw, produced Ibsen in Manchester, even when he was banned as indecent, and *Ghosts*, for instance, had to be performed "for members only". Eventually Miss Horniman became a casualty of Manchester's withdrawal into Cheshire. Her company did not carry enough 'big names' to draw the 'carriage folk' back into Manchester after dark, and many of them, like most theatre audiences, probably resented plays with a 'message' unless they were disguised as good entertainment.

Nevertheless it was the reputation for critical appreciation, earned in the Horniman era, that carried Manchester through the 1930s when it experienced its last theatrical glamour-time. The smaller companies visited the Princes Theatre, now pulled down, which was Manchester's most comfortable and elegant theatre, if my schoolboy memories of it are to be trusted. It was having a struggle to survive just before the 1939 war but at least it *had* survived. The 'Gaiety' had long been a cinema, plastered over with the most vulgar posters I had seen until the advent of supermarkets; the Ardwick 'Empire' had succumbed, the Manchester 'Hippodrome', home of variety and Pelissier's Follies, had become the Gaumont Cinema on Oxford Road. The Rusholme Repertory bravely tried to carry on a Horniman tradition but received precious little support. There was also the courageous experimentalism of the Unnamed Society, under the direction of the indomitable Frank Sladen-Smith. All the big shows went to the Opera House, Quay Street, or to the 'Palace', Oxford Road, inhabited, as it still mainly is, by pantomime from Christmas Eve until mid-March and for the rest of the year by variety and musicals.

But the nostalgia felt by the older generation today for the Manchester theatre of the thirties is almost wholly caused by the succession of brilliant shows—and they were brilliant—which had their world premières at the Opera House or the 'Palace' in that decade; shows like Noël Coward's *Bitter Sweet*, *Cavalcade* and *Operette*, and particularly the C. B. Cochran revues with their array of stars. To see these shows—it is always 'shows' of which that generation speaks, never plays—and then to dine at the 'Midland' or to have a drink beforehand in its Octagon Court, this was never-to-be-forgotten. That Manchester was accepting its theatre at second-hand from London didn't trouble the audiences in the least; after all, they were seeing these shows *before* London. It was blatant provincial one-upmanship. And eventually it almost killed the theatre in Manchester, because after the war the world of Cochran and Coward was as remote and ineffectual as the world of King Edward VII was after the First World War. No brilliant revues came to the Opera House; only the first night of *Oklahoma!* in 1947 came anywhere near the same standards, and it was played before an audience grown used to austerity in war and peace.

Gradually the audiences at the Opera House thinned out until now it is threatened with bingo or total closure unless the city council buys it. The 'Gaiety' was pulled down in the 1950s. The Rusholme Rep. failed to survive the war. The amateurs kept the flag flying and so did the companies at the Library Theatre, the tiny basement theatre in the Central Library run by the city council. Later came the comfortable small University Theatre, built in 1965 through the generosity of Sidney Bernstein of Granada, to seat a maximum of 361 for theatre in the round or 305 for proscenium productions. Mainly this houses university productions, and has been used for opera by the Royal Manchester College of Music. It has also been the temporary home of Manchester's most promising recent theatrical venture, the 69 Company.

This company has Michael Elliott, one of Britain's most thoughtful and sincere producers as its director, and its artistic aims have attracted people of the calibre of Tom Courtenay, Juliet Mills and Vanessa Redgrave to work for it at very low salaries. If it could build a theatre in Manchester it would make the city its permanent home and might well be the answer to the need for a new pattern of theatre in Manchester. In the meantime towns like Bolton with its splendid new Octagon Theatre take the lead.

Similar to the '69', and with the financial security of Granada Television behind it, is the Stables Theatre, a small theatre built in old stables near Granada's Quay Street headquarters. It is largely devoted to finding new plays and new authors, a policy that is bound to have a high percentage of failures and could never succeed without a Maecaenas in the offing. But splendid acting and imaginative production make the Stables and the '69' among the most distinguished provincial theatre ventures of recent years.

What, then, of those 'and-painted masterpieces in the City Art Gallery; how do the visual arts fare in Manchester? Their troubles began, with the best intentions, when the Royal Manchester Institution's building in Mosley Street became the City Art Gallery. It was probably inadequate for its purpose then, as most makeshifts are, and it certainly is now. The city's collection is in fact dispersed through six other galleries scattered round the suburbs, including the delightful Fletcher Moss Gallery at Didsbury, full of fine watercolours; the rich collection of English costume at Platt Hall, and moderns at Queen's Park. In the central gallery itself much of its space is regularly sacrificed to some temporary exhibition, and too often many of the finest items of the permanent collection are in the cellars.

For too long the amount of money allocated for the purchase of pictures by the city has been laughably low, therefore Manchester is rarely in the market for anything very exciting these days and consequently was taken aback in March 1970 when a superb Stubbs was suddenly acquired. But the collection is nevertheless distinguished: good examples of Sickert, Gauguin, Sisley and Boudin; some Constables; Reynolds's fine "Lord Hood"; David Cox's exquisite "Rhyl Sands" and some Epstein busts including his magnificent "C. P. Scott", a portrait of such commanding authority that one automatically prepares to address it as 'sir' (if one is a journalist, at any rate!).

But the crowning achievement is the assembly of pre-Raphaelites, their aggressive colours and pathological detail still taking the breath away. Here are Millais's "Autumn Leaves"; Madox Brown's "Work" (bought on C. P. Scott's recommendation for £400), the "Stages of Cruelty"; Holman Hunt's "Scapegoat", the "Light of the World" and "The Hireling Shepherd". Few paintings of women, it seems to me, contain a more truly seductive look in the eyes than that which Holman Hunt captured from Emma Watkins for "The Hireling Shepherd". How she got past the vigilance of the Victorian city fathers I will never know.

It is worth recalling, as one more example of the generosity of the city's benefactors, how Manchester acquired Barry's fine building, inadequate though it may now be despite the use of the Athenaeum alongside as an annexe. The Royal Manchester Institution had since its foundation concentrated on the arts rather than the literature and science it was also founded to sponsor. Each year it arranged exhibitions and began to buy contemporary paintings. It provided a home for the Manchester Academy of Fine Arts, founded in 1858, probably as a result of the enthusiasm for painting engendered by the great Art Treasures Exhibition. In 1882 the governors offered the building, the site it occupied and all its contents to the Corporation, free, stipulating only that the city should spend £2,000 a year for twenty years on buying works of art. Eventually, when thin times came, the city reduced that sum as soon as it legally could, a further example of civic pride coming a long way behind that shown by idealists like the original governors.

It was a private benefaction, from the will of the inventor and industrialist Sir Joseph Whitworth, that gave Manchester its other major art gallery, the Whitworth, built in Platt Park on the southern side of the city in 1895. Originally administered by a board of governors, the Whitworth is now the responsibility of the university, hence its small purchasing fund. But it has one of the best collections of English watercolours to be seen anywhere; and its recently modernised galleries make it one of the few places in the North where modern art can be seen in a proper setting. It owes much in every way to the work of a remarkable woman, Margaret Pilkington, who was its director for many years. In recent years smaller private galleries have been established in Manchester: even the Portico Library now shows pictures.

The city itself has not often been the subject for art. Yet it can claim a share in the development of a great and unique artist, because L. S. Lowry was a student at the Manchester School of Art—in his own words "a very uninspired student". Inspiration came to him when he was 23 and he missed the train to Manchester from Pendlebury station. Annoyed, he returned home and looked out of his window at a croft with a mill behind it and houses in front. It was a threatening day, with an intense light. He drew it, and for the next twenty years he drew little else except the industrial scene and its dark, shadowless men and women, like puppets, with thin legs and heavy boots, always in a crowd, leaving factories or going to football matches, yet each figure an individual carrying his private loneliness round him like a greatcoat. If anyone wants to know what Lancashire during the Depression looked like, they have to go to Lowry.

Until he was over 50 he painted without any real recognition from any source. "I often used to say to my mother, I think I'm a fool to keep on doing these things when nobody wants them. I'm filling the house with them." But in 1938 a London gallery-owner saw his work and showed it. Now people send Lowry reproductions as postcards. Salford has the biggest and best Lowry collection, Manchester hardly any. Where it could once have had them for a trifle, now it probably could not afford them.

Not that the curator of the City Art Gallery would have had an easy task getting his choice endorsed, in all probability. A frustrated group they must have been, Manchester's curators in the past thirty years. Whereas councillors would resent it if the curator publicly gave his views on the running of the waterworks or the transport department or the public baths, yet if the purchase of a picture comes up for debate almost every councillor turns into an uninhibited art critic, often, their utterances suggest, with the slightest possible acquaintance with the subject. Many of the public would like to see some aspects of new art in the gallery—Madox Brown, after all, was new art in 1882—and many find it as intolerable that city councillors should act as umpires in this matter as that they should have the power to decide which films are fit for the public to see.

To limit civic support of the arts is a short-sighted policy, and in the long run it insults the public. A writer in 1825, differing from the American quoted at the beginning of this chapter, said of Manchester, "the whole population seems to be imbued with a general thirst for knowledge and improvement". If this was true then, it was even truer later in the century when institutions and societies dedicated to lectures on almost every subject under the sun, swarmed throughout the area. Most famous of these, started in 1882, were the lectures and concerts organised by Charles Rowley and his Ancoats recreation committee, the 'Ancoats Brotherhood'. Rowley was a friend of the pre-Raphaelites and a particular friend of William Morris. He dedicated himself to bringing 'sweetness and light' into the lives of the poor of the Ancoats district. For next to nothing, Ancoats heard lectures by Bernard Shaw, by university professors, by leading politicians, they heard recitals by Busoni and quartets played by the renowned Brodsky Quartet. Though it is said that eventually the audience consisted of ladies and gentlemen from Bowdon and Fallowfield fashionably going slumming on a Sunday afternoon, there is no doubt of the good done by Rowley and similar men elsewhere. At Bolton, for example, from 1885 to 1913 a group met regularly to discuss the works and ideals of Walt Whitman.

Even if the subjects for enthusiasm were less exalted—such as the breeding of cage-birds or whippets—the seriousness and expertise betrayed the natural intelligence of Lancashire folk. Many societies and the extra-mural department of the university continue the tradition today, a tradition stemming from the mechanics' institutions, the lyceums, the working men's colleges established in Ancoats, Manchester and Salford in the late 1850s, the co-operative societies and the Workers' Educational Association. Nor must one overlook the impact of the first free library (1852), forerunner of the fine Central Library of today.

From the foregoing survey one common, binding factor emerges which has the largest bearing on Manchester's future as a city with more than pretensions to be regarded as the cultural capital of the North. There is no lack of activity in the arts in Manchester today, no lack of talent. But there is an apathy among the people which, if it is not eliminated, is the quickest way to kill enthusiasm and drive away talent. One way to eliminate it is to eliminate the common factor I have mentioned, which is the lack of the proper facilities in almost every area of artistic endeavour.

Only the Hallé has a really suitable home, for the Free Trade Hall, whatever its limitations, is still a good concert-hall and one which would be of even more use to the orchestra if the city council were to follow Liverpool's example and allow its use rent-free. The Art Gallery is too small, too old and run on a shoestring. Its only recent major modernisation—the rooms to house the superb Assheton-Bennett silver collection—was carried out only because the wealthy benefactress threatened to take the collection away if the proper setting was not provided, for most of which she herself then paid. There is no small central concert-hall in Manchester where recitalists or small instrumental groups can be heard to advantage and which could also house lectures and the meetings of amateur societies. The Free Trade Hall is too big for recitals, the Lesser Free Trade Hall is unsatisfactory in almost every way; this leaves Methodist churches or temperance halls or the Whitworth Hall of the university—all with drawbacks.

The city also needs a theatre of reasonable and realistic size economically and artistically, seating perhaps no more than 1,200. It needs—or does it?—an opera house, too. It has been promised one for years. Beecham, after his legendary performances of opera in Manchester in 1916 and 1917, offered to build one on the Piccadilly site and enthusiasts even then advocated a cultural centre containing opera house, art gallery, library and concert-hall. Beecham's offer, incidentally, opened with an imperious boast—"I will build in Manchester an opera house that shall be of size and importance not less than those of any other opera house in London or any continental towns with the exceptions of Paris and Petrograd." He then went bankrupt.

But the arts centre idea was revived in the euphoric post-war Manchester Plan of 1945 and again in the 1960s when the late Sir Maurice Pariser, a Labour alderman of the highest culture, propounded a costly scheme for an opera house, theatre and art gallery. The scheme was discussed and debated until the great 'squeeze and freeze' of Harold Wilson's second administration consigned it to a shelf. Pariser died, and no one has yet picked up the sword that fell from his hand.

In the form proposed his scheme was probably too ambitious. But a modified version of it may be a part of Manchester's future planning if it is still thought that an arts centre is the right answer. Or is it merely a tidy-minded planner's solution? Is it not a further example of the segregation, the pigeon-holing, that is a depressing feature of modern life? "He's an arts-lover, he'll go to the arts centre; I'm not, so I won't." This is the attitude to guard against. Might it not be better to provide the right buildings for the right events in different parts of the city, so that there is no fear of one large dead white elephant in its allotted paddock? One thing is certain: someone somewhere must take a decision and say "This is what we ought to do and we will do it." Seminars, conferences, sub-committees, democratic processes though they may be, are also the bureaucratic instruments of procrastination.

An opera house or arts centre would stand more chance if the maintenance of the arts in municipalities were to be removed once and for all from the area of local party politics and the rating system so that an end would be put to the shaming debates of whether money could be spared for the Hallé and the art gallery or whether it should be spent on housing and social services. The alternatives are unreal and false because they should never now be posed: the answer is that both are important for different reasons and both are essential. A city must have its hygiene and its humanities. Let no one be too harsh on Manchester City Council because, when expenditure had to be limited, it gave priority to re-housing, to social services and to education. The ghastly inheritance of the Industrial Revolution lay heavy on its conscience; much of it was there to see. I do not think that anyone who has walked through the worst areas of the city can say that the wrong choice was made. On the other hand, if waiting 'until the economic climate is right' is to be the yardstick, then that is equivalent to saying that major expenditure on the arts will never be undertaken.

But the old debate on whether the arts merit state and municipal support is over. They do. There should be a Treasury allocation of money for this purpose from a central national fund, and a city's only concern should be to see that it receives its full share, supplemented, one may still hope, by industry.

A system on these lines would also remove one of the criticisms which Manchester Corporation is entitled to make in reply to the brickbats labelled philistine which are constantly thrown at it. Its rateable area is comparatively small, yet its facilities are used by the towns throughout the conurbation. What support do wealthy Wilmslow or rich Bowdon or purse-proud Prestwich give to the Hallé, Manchester can ask. Perhaps £50 a year, perhaps nothing. Yet a large number of the ratepayers of these towns patronise most of Manchester's rate-subsidised cultural activities. These outlying towns are jealous of their independence, and Manchester for twenty years has fought a running battle with several of them who have resisted attempts to settle overspill on them. They can't eat their cake and have it, might well be the attitude in the Town Hall, Albert Square. It would also fall to Manchester's lot to bear the brunt of any increased expenditure on the extra transport that would be needed if an arts centre were to become a reality, because there would have to be an improvement in the facilities provided.

In the long run, it all depends on what Manchester's citizens want their city to be as the twenty-first century approaches. Not, surely, merely a workshop, dead at night. It is, of course, an exaggeration to say that it is dead at night now, just half-dead. But better facilities would breed better amenities—better restaurants, better car parks, better pubs. The trend, which the planning officer wishes to encourage, of bringing people back into Manchester to live is another essential towards the city's survival and revival. Where there is life there is support for activity, as the young people show in their basement clubs, whether one approves of them or not.

There is one final cogent reason why the Manchester of tomorrow must 'think big' on the arts, and must wipe out for ever the memory of the 1950 councillor who criticised "people like Barbirolli and Beecham" for having "big ideas", an attitude which typified the pusillanimous approach to civic responsibility that held Manchester back so disastrously in the decade from 1950–60. Manchester in the 1970s will be one of the largest educational centres in the world. The two universities, Manchester and

Salford, and the University Institute of Science and Technology, all expanding yearly; a new music college, built for over £1 million, magnificently equipped, with its own opera theatre and concert-hall, formed after long and painful gestation by the voluntary amalgamation of the Royal Manchester College of Music and the Northern School of Music; the amazingly courageous decision by Chetham's School to turn itself into the first full-time junior music school in the country; the greater concentration by Manchester Grammar School on subjects outside the normal scholastic curriculum in which it has such outstanding academic success; the Regional College of Art, also to have a splendid new building—what is the point of all this preparation for living if there is nothing at the end except improvisation, muddle and apathy?

EIGHT

THIS SPORTING LIFE

IT must not be thought, and I must not give the impression, that everybody in Manchester is concerned with the future of the arts or 'the idea of a city' in the way John Henry Newman was concerned with the idea of a university. Thousands of people in Manchester live full and happy lives who have never read a word of the *Guardian*, never set foot inside the Free Trade Hall, never heard a note played by the Hallé Orchestra, never tracked down a fact in the Central Library, never looked at a pre-Raphaelite painting and never regarded the Town Hall as anything but a place in which to pay the rates. (How often do you hear a *Coronation Street* character mention going to the Hallé or even to the theatre?) Yet Manchester has still had plenty to offer them, or perhaps in their case it would be truer to say the Manchester area. There are the clubs, of course. It has been said that Manchester in recent years has been famous the world over for its clubs, over 300 of them. Businessmen from London rarely ask to be taken to the Hallé: they want to sample 'the clubs' of which they have heard so much.

Gambling clubs, where thousands of pounds change hands in a few hours, strip clubs, sleazy clubs, clubs that ought to be closed and soon will be if the police have anything to say in the matter, clubs for the wealthy, clubs for the poor, working men's clubs, diners' clubs, loafers' clubs—Manchester has them all. They have taken the place of the music hall and in some respects of the pubs. At the best of them you can hear the top-line stars of the day— Frankie Howerd, Vera Lynn, Louis Armstrong—and dine and wine well; at another you can hear a band playing Glenn Miller's music in Glenn Miller's style, and playing it so well that Syd

Lawrence, the enthusiastic member of the Northern Dance Orchestra who began it, is now in demand all over the country. Perhaps some artistic amalgam of Lowry and Toulouse-Lautrec is at work recording club-life for subsequent generations.

Another place in which to see Manchester at play is Belle Vue. This Vanity Fair of entertainment is in Longsight. It has been there since 1836 when it was started as a pleasure garden in what was then a rather superior suburb. Now there are railway lines and a gas holder, depressingly old houses and a stream of traffic, but there is also still Belle Vue. It has a zoo, the speedway, go-kart racing, boxing, wrestling, an exhibition hall, merry-go-rounds, a big dipper, funfairs, gardens, the circus, dance-halls and dining suites. It is brash, vulgar, gregarious, but it is alive. Every year 6,000 people stream into the King's Hall to hear the Hallé perform *Messiah;* from 1944 to 1952 the King's Hall was the regular home of the Hallé's Sunday concerts. Sometimes the rain drummed on the roof, sometimes you could hear the lions roaring, sometimes a sparrow got in and chirped its accompaniment to Beethoven and Elgar, but Barbirolli and his players, in the circus-ring, made marvellous music there, for the place, whatever its drawbacks, had a special atmosphere that has never been recaptured elsewhere.

Here, too, the brass band championships are held. "Big blow at Belle Vue" is an old joke but it remains a good one. You need a Lancashire constitution to stand a brass band festival: perhaps a dozen or more bands playing the same test-piece, each band with its own style, drilled to perfection, aware of its competitors' strengths and weaknesses, determined to win the cup for the colliery or aviation works or co-operative society whose name it proudly bears. "Brass bands are all very well in their place—out of doors and about 20 miles away," Sir Thomas Beecham is said to have remarked. He wouldn't have dared to say it to Harry Mortimer or Eric Ball. In any case, staunch Lancastrian that he was, he must have known what superb musicians these bandsmen are and what the Hallé brass section owes to them. Only pigeon-fanciers can rival them for enthusiasm, but they are having a struggle to survive these days.

The tradition derives from the days when nearly every mill had its band; and every mill had its leading soprano, some weaver whose voice would be heard even over the noise of the looms. Singing at work, singing in chapel, singing, too, as a child in the

Looking towards the Cathedral High Altar

Whit Walks, the Sunday School processions begun in 1801 on Whit Monday when 1,800 Church of England schoolchildren gathered in St. Ann's Square and walked to t' owd church headed by the boroughreeve and a band. They have done it ever since, the Roman Catholics on another day in Whit week, and drivers had to put up with the delays while the children in their best frocks walked through the city. (Legend has it that the Sunday School teachers began the walks as a means of stopping parents taking their children to the races at Kersal.) But, of course, traffic has won, and now the Walks are held on a Saturday afternoon.

But the Manchester man's principal recreational activity today is, without doubt, watching football. Like Tyneside, like Liverpool, like Glasgow, Manchester is football-mad. It has two great teams to support, City and United, whose rival supporters regard each other with, at the best, scorn and, at the worst, bitter and bigoted hatred, because religion enters into it, United being the Roman Catholics' team and City the rest. The rivalry between the clubs under their two great managers, Sir Matt Busby and Joe Mercer, will no doubt one day be as garlanded with legend and anecdote as the 1920s rivalry of the Lancashire and Yorkshire cricket teams.

United came first. It was founded in 1878 when some workmen at the Lancashire and Yorkshire Railway locomotive repair shops in Newton Heath started a football club which they called the 'L and Y', with a ground at North Road. Later it became Newton Heath F.C. and played at Bank Street, Clayton. In 1909, as Manchester United, to which it had changed its name in 1901, the club moved to a ground in Old Trafford. Until 1939 its struggle was uphill. During the war the ground was severely damaged, but in 1945 the far-seeing directors appointed as manager a Scotsman, Matt Busby, who, ironically, had played for Manchester City.

The rest is as familiar and as illustrious a story as Barbirolli's Hallé, with which it runs almost parallel. In 1948 United won the F.A. Cup at a classic Wembley Final with a side, led by Johnny Carey, that many good judges regard as the best the club has had. But it was not a young side and Busby looked to the future. He did not rely on his cheque-book to import star players by the transfer system, but sent out scouts to watch school sides throughout the district. Promising players were put on the

Fletcher Moss Gallery, once the Old Parsonage, Didsbury

Pupils on their way to Manchester Grammar School

United books at Old Trafford and given expert coaching. Inevitably they became known as the Busby Babes, and they soon justified his policy, winning the First Division League Championship in 1952. During the 1950s Busby built up a superb young side, including Duncan Edwards, Bobby Charlton, Tommy Taylor (a £30,000 transfer from Barnsley), Mark Jones, Dennis Viollet, David Pegg, Eddie Colman, Albert Scanlon, Jackie Blanchflower, Roger Byrne, Johnny Berry and Ray Wood. Each player was outstanding; the writer and former Arsenal player Bernard Joy said in 1956 that after another three years in which to mature, this side would be "strong claimants for the unofficial title of greatest English club side of all time". League champions in 1955–6 and 1956–7, they were also Cup Finalists at Wembley in 1957 when they were beaten by Aston Villa.

In the 1956–7 season United also invaded international football by entering the European Cup, a venture that was at first frowned upon by the Football League authorities who believed that it would involve a club in too many matches. Nevertheless Busby went ahead and the team reached the semi-final, when they were defeated by Real Madrid. Having won the English League championship they were eligible to compete in the 1957–8 European competition. On 5th February 1958 they met Red Star of Jugoslavia in the second leg of the quarter-final. United had won the first leg at Old Trafford in January. The second leg was a 3–3 draw. Next day United left Belgrade for home. Their Elizabethan aircraft refuelled at Munich. The weather was wintry and the pilot made two fruitless attempts to take off. On the third attempt the plane lifted off the runway but hit some buildings on the edge of the airfield and burst into flames. Twenty-one people were killed and ten seriously injured.

The news reached Britain during the late afternoon and the crash assumed the proportions of a national tragedy. To this day the word Munich means only one thing in Manchester—the United air crash, not the political event of 1938. No one who was in the city on the evening of that cold February day or the next morning is ever likely to forget it. It was a city of mourning, and the buildings, which were then mostly still black, merely provided the right backcloth for the scenes of tragedy in the streets. No one smiled in Manchester that week. Strangers commiserated with one another. People who had never watched a football match in their lives still felt bereft and were moved by the thought of the golden lads who had come so swiftly and violently to dust and ashes at the height of their youthful vigour and skill. Nor was football the only sufferer. Manchester's newspaper population is second only to Fleet Street's, and eight journalists had perished.

Cynics eventually criticised the extraordinary expressions of grief and sympathy which accompanied the Munich disaster; after all, there had been other air crashes. Was one death more tragic than another? Of course not; but this particular example of sudden death perhaps brought home to thousands, as other crashes could not unless one knew one of the victims personally, the risks run in the cause of public entertainment. Football, like it or not, is part of national life (it was a Manchester news editor who said in 1940, when France fell, "Now we're in t'Final"); football players are household words. And the United team of the 1950s were not only local heroes, they were renowned for their deeds throughout Europe.

There was an extra poignancy in the knowledge that United really were a team, not a collection of stars assembled from other teams. Most of them had played together for several years, had trained as boys together. Now they had died together. No wonder the people of Manchester collectively felt stunned by the news that came in on 6th February 1958: Roger Byrne, dead; Tommy Taylor and Dave Pegg, inseparables on and off the field, dead; Geoff Bent, Eddie Colman, Mark Jones, Bill Whelan, all dead; Jackie Blanchflower and Johnny Berry so badly injured that they would never play football again; Duncan Edwards, the youngest player to win an England cap, probably the finest footballer of a generation, fought for his life for a fortnight but died; Walter Crickmer, secretary of the club for thirty-two years and its wisest counsellor, dead; Tom Curry and Bert Whalley, trainers, both dead; Matt Busby so gravely injured that there were despair for his life and constant rumours of his death; Alf Clarke (*Evening Chronicle*), George Follows (*Daily Herald*), H. D. Davies ('Old International' of the *Manchester Guardian*), Henry Rose (*Daily Express*), Tom Jackson (*Manchester Evening News*), Archie Ledbrooke (*Daily Dispatch*), Eric Thompson (*Daily Mail*) and Frank Swift (*News of the World*), all dead. Bobby Charlton, Albert Scanlon, Ray Wood, Harry Gregg, Ken Morgans, Dennis Viollet and Bill Foulkes had minor injuries only

Gregg, the goalkeeper, went back into the blazing aircraft to rescue some of his companions.

The conventional expressions of sympathy, the memorial services, the obituaries, were moving tributes in themselves. But perhaps the most impressive aftermath was at Old Trafford on the evening of 19th February. United were still in the F.A. Cup and due to meet Sheffield Wednesday. To strengthen what had to be a new team, and was in any case an emotionally shattered team, Ernie Taylor of Blackpool and Stan Crowther of Aston Villa were transferred to United. They played on the 19th, so did Foulkes and Gregg. Two other players had never before played in the first team, the remainder were reserves. Yet United won 3–0, and there is little doubt that this was the doing of the United supporters, whose passionate, almost hysterical intensity that evening was of an order rarely encountered. Massed willpower won the match. Incredibly, United went on to reach the Final of the Cup, where they were defeated by Bolton Wanderers.

Busby, restored to health by the skill of the surgeons at the Rechts der Isar Hospital, Munich, returned to build a new side. This great man rarely speaks of Munich, and one senses that part of him is permanently in mourning for the players he lost there. Cheerfully and indomitably he created another United, a different team in character and ability from its predecessor, a team for the 'swinging sixties', extroverts all, or nearly all, a hard-playing team on and off the field. Its stars have included Viollet, Quixall, Pearson, Herd, Setters and four outstandingly brilliant players: the mercurial Scotsman Denis Law; the Irish genius George Best; the aggressive and rugged wing-half Norbert Stiles; and Bobby Charlton, a great sportsman and gentleman, in temperament and outlook the football equivalent of the cricketer Brian Statham.

This side, cheered on by fanatical supporters whose lunatic fringe has brought disgrace to Manchester football by moronic acts of hooliganism, won the F.A. Cup, the Football League and, on a never-to-be-forgotten night at Wembley in May 1968, the European Cup. When Matt Busby, by then a C.B.E., a Freeman of Manchester and soon to be a knight, walked out on to the pitch it was for him a memorial act of homage as much as a moment of triumph.

Some football-minded sociologist, which I am not, will perhaps analyse the three 'Busby Uniteds': the indomitables of the '40s, the immortals of the '50s and the inimitables of the '60s. In their individual histories can be traced footballers' increasing personal rewards. What would the stalwarts of Newton Heath in the 1890s think about Georgie Best, the long-haired symbol of his generation, with his fantastic ability on the field, his string of boutiques catering for the tastes of the younger generation in all their colourful eccentricity, his Jaguar cars, his feminine admirers, his £30,000 house in Bramhall?

If United's name has a mystique that naturally stems from success, tragedy and the outstanding personality of its manager, Manchester City at Maine Road has equal claim on the devotion of its supporters. It began life as West Gorton F.C. in 1880, became Ardwick F.C. with a ground at Hyde Road, and changed into Manchester City in 1894. The famous Meredith was City's bright particular star and helped them to their first F.A. Cup, although he and four other City players eventually joined United as a result of a scandal concerned with improper payments.

City have had many other great players but none more beloved than their goalkeeper Frank Swift, 'Big Swiftie', a gentle giant, who died as a newspaperman at Munich. I remember a wartime international at Maine Road against Scotland, in 1942 or 1943, from which two sights have stayed clear in my mind for nearly thirty years: the sleight-of-foot of Stanley Matthews and the amazing goalkeeping of Frank Swift, his huge hand picking up the ball as if it had been a marble. Today City, too, have a wise and tolerant manager in Joe Mercer, Best-type stars in Mike Summerbee, Colin Bell, Francis Lee and Tony Book. F.A. Cup winners and League champions in the late sixties, League Cup winners in 1970, their star is in the ascendant.

These sportsmen are part of the warp and woof of the city's life, their deeds carved into Manchester's history as the figures of Agricola and others are carved into the fabric of the Town Hall. And nowhere has the richness of Lancashire life, its humour and character, been more sharply characterised than on the county cricket ground at Old Trafford. Like the Hallé, Old Trafford is the direct outcome of the Art Treasures Exhibition. Manchester Cricket Club's ground was at Stretford; its site was part of the area commandeered in 1856 for the erection of the exhibition pavilion. The club were furious and fought the eviction order but to no avail. They found another ground only a few yards away and played their first match on it against Liverpool, winning by 31 runs. Thus was Old Trafford inaugurated. In 1864, when the county club was formed, Manchester's ground became its headquarters. In the years since then it has been the scene of many great and memorable games and the home of innumerable superb players.

Francis Thompson's "my Hornby and my Barlow long ago" were Lancashire's opening pair in the 1880s, the autocratic amateur captain A. N. Hornby and the archetype professional R. G. Barlow. They were legends in their lifetimes, but they were succeeded by legends, A. C. MacLaren, R. H. Spooner, J. T. Tyldesley, the elegant Edwardians of Lancashire cricket, with Walter Brearley the Falstaff to MacLaren's Prince Hal. Then, between the wars, the character of the team changed, though not its proportion of characters. If MacLaren and Spooner represent the Manchester of the cotton boom, of Richter at the Hallé and Brodsky at the College, the team of the 1920s, with fewer amateurs able to spare time to play, represents an industrial equivalent of the age of Noël Coward, the flappers and Oxford bags, and the team of the 1930s matched the mood of a county on the dole: grimly good-humoured and determined, dour and undaunted.

Fortunately the Lancashire teams of those years enjoyed the rare privilege of having their deeds and characters chronicled by the game's greatest writer, Neville Cardus, born in a poor home in the suburbs of Manchester in 1889, self-educated, a lover of music and cricket and literature, a man with a Dickensian appreciation of the quirks and eccentricities of his fellow humans. From 1919–39 he reported cricket for the *Manchester Guardian*, and his books on the subject long ago became classics. It is sometimes said that he himself 'created' the characters of the Lancashire team of the 1920s, and while Sir Neville himself would be the last to deny the charge he would also be the first to claim that he was provided with rich and rare raw material.

"Sing as we go and let the world go by," sang Gracie Fields; and if Cecil Parkin, Dick Tyldesley, George Duckworth, McDonald and Hallows never let the world go by so far as cricket was concerned, one of them, Parkin, did literally sing as he walked back to bowl. Parkin was the hero of many Cardus anecdotes, but

I was once able to tell Sir Neville a Parkin story he did not know, told to me by one of Parkin's drinking cronies. One season, about 1925 or 1926, a young amateur from the South was having a brilliant run of success with the bat, either approaching 1,000 runs in May or several centuries in succession, something of that nature. To achieve his record, success in his innings against Lancashire was essential. When Parkin came on to bowl, the magic figure was within reach. As Lancashire's captain, Leonard Green, handed Parkin the ball he said, "Go easy on him, he's a young man and it would be splendid for him to make those runs." Parkin took up the tale, in his high-pitched voice: "So I bowled 'im long hops on leg and 'e hit me for four, and full-tosses outside off-stump and 'e hit them for fours too. 'E got to his record score and all crowd stood and we all shook 'is hand. Then I went up to skipper and said 'Can I bowl 'im out now, Mr. Green?' I bowled 'im next ball—I could 've bowled 'im with a ruddy balloon."

The late H. D. Davies described Cardus as "the Victor Trumper of cricket writers, for they both had five strokes to everyone else's one". Lancashire cricket missed Cardus after 1945, but he would have found fit drama for his pen as he watched Lancashire in its lean years, struggling to find its soul again. The great players were there—Washbrook, Ikin, Pollard, Tattersall, Ken Grieves, Ken Cranston, Malcolm Hilton, Ken Higgs and, best of all, J. B. Statham, most accurate and graceful of modern fast bowlers and most unaffected of men—but the side lacked cohesion. Now it is reaching another peak, thanks to Bond, Pilling and the bespectacled West Indian Clive Lloyd, who walks out to bat like a professor whose feet are hurting him—until he reaches the crease.

The glory of Old Trafford is that it has the air of a country ground. Though the electric trains pass by every ten minutes, their passengers craning to see the scoreboards, though the tall buildings of Manchester loom up 2 miles away, there is nothing about cricket at Old Trafford which seems alien to the surroundings, as for example cricket at The Oval seems out of place, an intruder. Old Trafford resembles Lord's in its capacity to exist entirely for itself and for the game. The student of the Manchester character should never pass up the chance to sit in a great crowd at Old Trafford: he will hear wit there, bawdy humour, common sense and extraordinary knowledge of the game. Cardus long ago specified the difference between a Lancashire and a Yorkshire cricket crowd:

> When Lancashire collapses the Old Trafford crowd will simply curse the county players heartily for a while and ease its heart that way. But at Leeds one afternoon, when Yorkshire collapsed against Notts, though the crowd took a rather lasting sorrow with it to tea, no word of complaint or distrust was uttered against Yorkshire cricket.

It is true that, in common with all other English grounds, Old Trafford has known play to be stopped by rain, but one's abiding memories of it are of sunshine, a clear light, and the run-stealers flickering to and fro. It is not really surprising that Lancashire cricket should have inspired both the best cricket poem and the best cricket prose; and also a superb example of double-edged feminine wit when Statham's wife, on hearing that Brian had been made a C.B.E., said that it stood for Cricket Before Everything.

Less than a mile from Old Trafford is the Cheshire border. This proximity of Cheshire, primarily an agricultural county, to Manchester has been of important historical and social significance to the city and the source of a good deal of acrimony. Cheshire is Manchester's playground and the home of a good many Mancunians. It is a perpetual source of surprise to the unknowing and unsuspecting how quickly the Mancunian can escape from the city into the green of the countryside.

It is in Cheshire that one encounters the social snobberies and distinctions that, in their multiplicity and variety, have survived all attempts to iron them out into a dull egalitarianism. Cheshire has dukes and earls, and a Home Counties outlook. It is a very rich county, some say the richest in England. A leading London dress designer told me that his wealthiest customers came from Cheshire. You can see polo played in Cheshire, its hunt ball is a social event on the grand scale; property prices are astronomical in some areas. Houses costing over £20,000 are common in the area around Wilmslow, Alderley Edge and Prestbury, three of Cheshire's strongholds of what one might call the Campari belt.

Dining in Cheshire is a favourite Mancunian pastime, for the county is rich in country inns which specialise in good food. The fashion swings from one to another and back again. Knutsford, Mobberley, Peover—each can offer sophisticated pleasures. The

meaning of Cheshire is best defined by the single hard fact that
the exact counterpart of the house which costs £4,000 in Lancashire can cost you £8,000 in Cheshire.

How much of Cheshire life is centred on Chester, that once
beautiful city which has now almost lost its character through the
assaults of developers, architectural vandals and sheer neglect, and
how much on Manchester is debatable. The 'Cheshire set' are not
much seen in Manchester. (The Wirral, the northern peninsula of
Cheshire, seems a world alien from the rest of the county, with a
life of its own owing allegiance to Liverpool and Birkenhead.)
The most indigenously Mancunian area of Cheshire is probably
Bowdon, an attractive leafy suburb, which still manages to retain
an air of leisure and opulence even though many of its villas are
flats now. There's still plenty of money in Bowdon, but it is
money made in Manchester and likely still to be spent in Manchester. In this respect it differs from Wilmslow, which is a
stopping-place on the main railway line to London. The Wilmslow wives can almost as easily go to London for their clothes as
to King Street. Their husbands are Manchester-based, no doubt,
but their work takes them often to London, via the morning
Pullman. It is almost a cliché of Manchester life to describe the
assembly of luxurious cars left at Wilmslow station like a daily
Motor Show. It was a sight for the social historian in the 1930s;
it still is today.

If Cheshire is the rich man's social playground it also provides
plenty of other attractions of perhaps more general and lasting
value and pleasure. Boating on the meres, the beautiful villages of
Gawsworth and Pott Shrigley, motor-racing at Oulton Park,
horse-racing on the Roodee, a day at Tatton Park, Knutsford, the
most frequently visited of all National Trust properties, some of
the best and most picturesque village cricket still to be found—
these all have their place in a portrait of Manchester, for they are
part of the Manchester man's way of life. It is hardly surprising
that the planners, seeking sites for new satellite towns of 'overspill'
population, should have thought that Cheshire would provide
them. But in one place after another a costly battle was fought,
with the Cheshire townsmen determined to repel the city
invaders. Mobberley, Lymm, Wilmslow—each plainly told
Manchester "You're not wanted here." The idea of a Greater
Manchester Authority with jurisdiction over areas of Cheshire

will be fought, it is plain, to a standstill. Infiltration is one thing, takeover quite another. That Manchester has come to acknowledge this was borne out by its abandonment, in July 1970, of its overspill schemes. Cheshire's case has been based not, as the county's critics have said, solely on the desire to maintain a middle-class enclave, but on the belief that Manchester was not making enough use of the waste land within its own boundaries and was committing ratepayers and taxpayers to enormous and unnecessary expense.

There's another aspect of Manchester's recreational life that must find its place here, apart from the esoteric fact that it has a flourishing following for real tennis. Many a Mancunian poring over his office papers during the week is transformed into a bronzed outdoor Apollo at the weekends. There is a special light in his eyes as he strides through the streets. Inevitably, he is one of those who recharges his urban batteries by walking in the Peak District. Millers Dale, Edale, Hayfield, Kinder Scout, the Snake, the Goyt Valley, Jacob's Ladder, Wildboarclough, these are the names which are as musical to his ears as are Hornby and Barlow to the *aficionado* of cricket. And it is not only walking that Derbyshire offers, but gliding and the terrifying but totally enslaving sport of pot-holing. When it comes to playing, the Mancunian sometimes finds hard ways of doing it, and I don't only mean Rugby League.

NINE

NEWS AND VIEWS

How many people in Manchester or elsewhere today know the name Alderman W. T. Jackson? Very few, I imagine; yet he was the originator of one of Manchester's most imaginative and progressive modern developments, which grew from the post-war re-housing crisis of 1919. In that year the short-lived Addison Act empowered local authorities, within a strict procedure of control and inspection by the new Ministry of Health, to provide new homes aided by a government grant for schemes which exceeded the proceeds of a penny rate. It was also the age of suburban development. Where a hundred years before only the wealthy with carriages could live outside the city, now buses, trams and trains gave the same chance to everyone.

Manchester decided to look beyond its suburbs, if necessary, for room to expand; and in March of 1919 W. T. Jackson proposed the building of three garden-city estates. But where? Land to the east and west of Manchester was built-up, to the north the available land was bleak, the smoke from the city drifted there, people didn't want to live there; but to the south, over the Mersey, was a land flowing with milk and honey—2,500 acres of woodlands, green fields, a timbered old hall, no smoke, easily accessible. Moreover it could be bought for £80 an acre instead of £400 in the city area. Its name was the Wythenshawe estate. Mr. Jackson had walked there in 1918 and dreamed of it as a garden city for industrial workers.

There were two snags. The estate belonged to the Tatton family; and it was in Cheshire. The Tatton family wouldn't sell, but the head of the family conveniently died and his heir was prepared to come to terms. Whereupon the city council's ruling

123

party decided not to buy, but only by a narrow majority. It was at this point, in 1926, that private action put a Trojan Horse into the estate.

Ernest Simon and his wife Shena—he a wealthy industrialist, she an educationist and social worker, both to the Left in politics and a former Lord Mayor and Lady Mayoress—bought Wythenshawe Hall and its 250 acres of land and presented them unconditionally to the city. The council had a second vote and decided to buy the rest of the estate. Now began a three-year battle while Manchester promoted a private Bill to bring Wythenshawe and 5,500 other acres of Cheshire into the city's administrative boundary. Cheshire, Manchester ratepayers and the rural district councils fought hard to defeat the scheme but the Bill became law in 1930, and the Wythenshawe project went ahead under the architectural leadership of Barry Parker, who had designed Hampstead garden suburb and Letchworth.

It was a daring and advanced concept, and town planners from all over the world came to see what Manchester was doing. It began as a town of 10,000 houses. Today, 102,000 people live in Wythenshawe in 23,000 council houses and 4,400 private houses. Its parks and tree-lined roads, insisted upon by Shena Simon despite criticism of the expense involved, proved that the planners' most high-minded blueprints could be translated into reality. But Wythenshawe's problems derived from one inescapable fact: that planners cannot plan people. 'Neighbourhood planning', each 'unit' separated by a green belt, looks splendid to the visiting town planner, but to the people who lived there it often meant loneliness, isolation and a sense of living in a place with no soul.

It was soon realised that a mistake had been made, that the place needed a social centre, but financial crises and a second World War bedevilled all extra expenditure on Wythenshawe. For years it seemed to the visitor from other parts of Manchester to be a place apart, difficult to find your way in, full of dead ends and roads that looked exactly like each other. People who moved there said it took them two years to find their way about, there were long walks to bus stops, and long journeys to work unless you were one of the 60 per cent employed at factories on the estate, chief among them Ferranti, A.E.I. and Timpson's Shoes.

In 1969, forty years after the estate plan had begun to take shape, the foundation stone was laid of a civic centre, designed to graft a 'living heart' on to a body noted for hardening of the arteries and chilly circulation. The centre will contain a library with an initial £100,000 stock, a small theatre, two swimming pools, indoor recreational facilities including a large sports hall, and a public hall. A restaurant and bar will serve all comers. Whether this £1,300,000 experiment will succeed in giving Wythenshawe its long-sought civic identity can only be known twenty years hence.

If the inhabitants do not use the amenities of the centre, it will merely add to the sense of sterility in the place, and there will be further work for the social workers in trying to combat vandalism and all the other manifestations of boredom. Private enterprise is pinning its hopes on other planned developments: twenty-four clubs, thirty-five pubs, thirty-two churches, one hundred shops in a new town centre. If both public and private enterprise succeed, Wythenshawe will have justified Alderman Jackson's walk across the Tatton estate.

I began this chapter with Wythenshawe because it epitomises the continuing interplay in Manchester between idealism and practicality, materialism and liberalism. It also served to introduce two remarkable individuals who may be taken as archetypes of a particular brand of Mancunian enterprise and activity. The Simons' labours for Manchester extended over the best part of fifty years. Housing, education, the university, smoke abatement, local government—in all these fields the Simons laboured. Unlike the Webbs, they laboured often in separate fields, only occasion-ally together; like the Webbs they absorbed statistics and blue books like meat and drink; like the Webbs, too, they remained aloof from the sort of people whose interests they had at heart.

Ernest Simon was born in 1879, nineteen years after his father Henry, a Prussian, had arrived in Manchester, where he eventually founded the great engineering firms of Henry Simon Ltd. and Simon Carves Ltd., now amalgamated into the Simon Engine-ering Group. Henry Simon died in 1899. (He was one of the three businessmen who founded the Hallé Concerts Society, and I was told by Hans Richter's daughter that the deciding factor in her father's acceptance of the Hallé conductorship in 1899 was his affection for Simon.)

Ernest was pitched early into industrial responsibility, for which he had natural business aptitude and a highly developed sense of social responsibility. Born in Lady Bracknell's "purple of commerce", he had the wealth to allow him to indulge his passion for social science, and he was aware of how vulnerable this made him to his opponents. All his life he wore a moral hair-shirt: he was terrified of self-indulgence because he was no prig and enjoyed good food and expensive holidays. In his youth he played polo to keep fit, but his pleasure was spoiled by the thought that £500 a year to keep the ponies was an extravagance.

He confided his self-searching to his diary under headings like "My qualities", "My defects", "My achievements". He knew that his shyness—which had helped to build a barrier of reserve between him and his father—was often interpreted as brusqueness, and he resolved one new year "to drop my superior, contemptuous and aggravating way of snubbing people who seem to me wrong, and to make a real effort to be interested in everybody". This makes him sound like an unsocial Socialist, and if he had no time for you he was. For most of his life he was a Liberal, although naturally drawn to Socialist doctrine and dogma. (Yet I suspect that at heart he remained a private-enterprise capitalist.) His view of people as members of groups, as 'citizens' with 'a duty to the community' rather than as irrational human beings, was typically Socialist. He invariably acted for the best, in his lights, but failed to understand that not everyone was as high-minded as he. How could anyone be happy simply doing nothing, he would ask. It was beyond him.

Yet he respected individuals. He infallibly picked the best men to run his business and gave them their heads, without interference. He refused to join the Labour Party after 1919 because, among other things, one of his companies dealt with collieries to whose owners the idea of nationalisation was repellent. As trustee for the Simon family, he felt he could not imperil the firm's future by his own beliefs. In politics he himself followed the predictable pattern of influences of his type—the Webbs, Tawney, Fabian and Liberal summer schools, Keynes, a visit to Moscow in the 1930s and, at the end of his days, Bertrand Russell and the Campaign for Nuclear Disarmament. (Three of his brothers had died in the 1914–18 war.) The passions of his life were housing and education, and it was for these that he strove hardest and achieved most.

He was perhaps happiest in the work he did for Manchester

University. As chairman of its council alongside its great Vice-Chancellor, John Stopford, he had pioneered the doubling of its student population within the eleven years from 1939 to 1950. It is principally to him that Manchester owes the reflected glory from the fame of the university's radio telescope at Jodrell Bank, near Holmes Chapel, Cheshire. He encouraged expenditure on the project even when it was £200,000 overspent and the Commons Public Accounts Committee expressed disapproval on the taxpayers' behalf. When an appeal was launched, the Simon firms contributed £20,000. Sir Bernard Lovell must have been a happy man knowing that his ambitions to give Britain an outstanding scientific instrument were backed against all comers by the chairman of his university.

There were two barren episodes in Ernest Simon's long life. One was his experience as M.P. for Withington from 1923–4. Parliament was not his milieu, whereas the council committee was. He was horrified, naturally, by "politicians who care more for votes than for principles". What is more, again naturally, he found the House of Commons thoroughly inefficient. Installing a Speaker, for instance, wasted a whole week. Members had to scramble for seats, whereas every city council provided its members with a desk and a comfortable seat. "In Parliament, the lack of a desk for papers causes very grave loss of time and efficiency," he wrote.

Equally frustrating were his five years as chairman of the B.B.C. from 1947–52. The Director-General was a Manchester acquaintance, William Haley, a former editor of the *Manchester Evening News* and later to be editor of *The Times*. In Haley, Simon met his match. He used words like "icy" and "granite resistance" to describe their relationship. "Haley is a colleague and opponent worthy of all one has, if he could be humanised," Simon wrote. He was evidently unconscious of any irony.

Simon joined the Labour Party in 1945 and entered the House of Lords as Lord Simon of Wythenshawe. In November 1959, just after his eightieth birthday, he received the Freedom of Manchester, and in his speech at the ceremony he surveyed the city council's work since 1838, giving credit for three outstanding achievements, the waterworks, the Ship Canal and Wythenshawe. He also attacked London for its failure to recognise the importance of Manchester "as a northern capital city" and for its "assumption of superior wisdom and concentration of power" which were "inimical to local responsibility and init-iative".

Simon had always been worried by the desertions of potential leaders from the provinces to London and his chief aim in working for Manchester was to make it attractive enough for these desertions to be rendered unnecessary. Although he did not inherit his father's interest in music, he wrote "as a devoted citizen of Manchester" to Barbirolli in 1948 when the Hallé conductor refused a tempting offer to leave Manchester for the B.B.C. Symphony Orchestra:

> I think the pressure on the best people in every walk of life to go to London is almost a disaster to our provincial centres, and your example . . . should also be a real stimulus to the cultural life of the great provincial centres in other ways. I refrain from giving my views as chairman of the B.B.C.!

The development in his sense of humour was caused by his happy marriage to Shena Potter (Beatrice Webb's maiden name was also Potter, but the two women were unrelated except spiritually). Shena was handsome, intelligent and a graduate of the London School of Economics. A friend who knew she would be the right wife for Ernest Simon introduced them. On their honeymoon in 1912 she read the report of the Royal Commission on Divorce while Ernest wrote light-hearted limericks: the fact that he wanted to do so was signal evidence of the effect Shena had on his character. He mellowed under her influence. She preceded him by ten years into the Labour Party, and when he joined her there he wrote her a long statement of his political faith, ending "With all my love, darling wife—and soon to be 'comrade' ".

Shena Simon is perhaps an even more remarkable personality than her husband, to whom she acted as a catalyst. Courageous she always was, and needed to be, because she did her best work at a time when a woman's participation in civic affairs was still resented. Operating from within a privileged social position she encountered much misunderstanding of her motives. Her extreme intelligence and strongly-held views aroused resentful antagon-isms, as did her strong and militant feminism in the suffragette campaigns.

The CIS building, highest in Manchester

She joined her husband on the city council in 1924, becoming a distinguished chairman of the education committee in 1932. Her actions and views were altogether too radical for the Conservatives, who made a determined effort to ensure her defeat in the 1933 municipal elections and succeeded. She joined the Labour Party in 1935, and though she never regained her council seat she was co-opted as a member of the education committee. A champion of children and teachers, opposed to any cuts in expenditure on education and to inequalities of opportunity, she still served on the committee in her eighties. In 1964, she too, was made a Freeman of the city.

These are the outlines of the careers of the Simons of Wythenshawe. What can never be fully assessed is the influence on a city of two people of their calibre, dedicated to the idea of public service, however misguided their opponents may have thought that service to be. This influence is wielded on one level on the floor of the council chamber or in the pages of a pamphlet; on another, and perhaps more potent level, it is purveyed by the act of being host and hostess. The Simons' house, Broomcroft, in Didsbury, was a sphere of influence of the kind in which provincial life is particularly rich. And nowhere was richer in these spheres of influence than Didsbury: Gustav Behrens at 'Holly Royde', Leonard Behrens at 'Netherby', Philip Godlee at 'The White House, all in different ways provided a focus for varying shades of thought and action.

Inevitably the phrase 'the Didsbury set' was coined to denote the Mancunian Establishment. It is objected to in Didsbury because of its implication that its alleged members acted as some kind of organised group. Of course they did, and why deny it? People who lived near each other, worked near each other, shared views or shared powers, quite naturally saw a lot of each other in their homes. As an influential force it has existed for a hundred years, firmly based on the *Manchester Guardian*, the university, the textile industry, social science and politics, with the arts in some cases a binding though rarely a determining factor.

Didsbury itself has contributed something to this phenomenon. Though so firmly within the city boundary, it is still known as 'the village' and has miraculously kept something of a village atmosphere amid the urban surroundings. The description of it as "the Hampstead Garden Suburb of the North-West" is accurate

Hulme before rehousing began

As it is today

in more ways than one. Overlooking the Mersey meadows it has still a rural air; its cricket ground, its church, its most famous pub, all carry a flavour of pastoral isolation. The Fletcher Moss art gallery, formerly The Old Parsonage, is a delightful building, inside and out. Didsbury's roads are lined with trees and flowering shrubs; names like Elm Road, Pine Road, The Beeches, emphasise this arboreal beauty; then there are Lapwing Lane, Ford Lane and, as a reminder that the Mersey is near, Fog Lane. Its central artery is Palatine Road, intersected by Barlow Moor Road. Fallowfield and Withington, two other favoured suburbs, are practically conjoined with Didsbury yet each retains a separate identity. It is a very pleasant area in which to live.

If, for the sake of convenience, we take Ernest and Shena Simon in their heyday as the centre of this influential sphere, it can be seen how much radiated from them to make up a vital constituent element in Mancunian life at its peak of grandeur. For the advantage of provincial social-intellectual life over that of the capital is that whereas it may numerically and even individually be smaller and less impressive, it is far more concentrated, far more readily accessible to willing participants. At Broomcroft you could meet the university professors, the industrialists like Charles Renold, the *Guardian*'s editor and some of his staff. The Mancunian family dynasties, Scotts, Simons, Behrenses, congregated there and put the world, the flesh and the devil to rights according to good Liberal principles.

To the outsider, or the Tory (carefully 'screened' before admittance) it could all seem overpowering, stifling even, and jokes about "the importance of being Ernest" made a wry sense. Mrs. Rachel Ryan, a granddaughter of C. P. Scott, has written elsewhere of how, in her childhood, she was free from any kind of racial prejudice because in Manchester, then as now, one grew accustomed to one's friends being Jews or Germans or both, or Armenians or Turks, but to be a Tory—now, that was the stigma of uncleanness. A nice girl didn't play with Tory children. It was all very high-minded and progressive; and it was not without an insufferable element of smugness and of intellectual snobbery.

If one seeks the unifying factor in the great days of Mancunian ascendancy, intellectual and commercial, it is perforce the *Manchester Guardian*, and in particular C. P. Scott's *Manchester Guardian*—which may be said to have continued to exist for about fifteen years after his death in 1932. Scott was appointed editor in 1872 at the age of 25 by his cousin John Edward Taylor II, the paper's proprietor. He had been born in Bath and completed his education at Oxford with a First in Greats. The industrial North was foreign ground to him yet he threw himself wholeheartedly and immediately into its problems.

He came of a family of dissenters, and an identification with minority views was bred into him. From his first day in its editorial chair he was determined to turn the *Manchester Guardian* from an ailing local newspaper into an international influence, and he did it by working himself and his staff inexorably. He knew how to pick writers, and gradually he obtained first-rate men to write about theatre, music, the visual arts and a host of other subjects. For example, George Saintsbury, Adolphus Ward, Comyns Carr, Arthur Evans, York Powell, Richard Jefferies, James Bryce, H. W. Nevinson, J. M. Synge, Arthur Johnstone, R. C. K. Ensor, C. E. Montague, L. T. Hobhouse, W. T. Arnold, James Agate, Ernest Newman, Oliver Elton, Samuel Langford, Herbert Sidebotham and Allan Monkhouse all wrote for Scott's *Guardian* before the First World War. He did not like commissioning articles from non-staff contributors—Shaw, for example —"because when we get them we may not like them."

The *Guardian* had been a daily paper since 1855. It was at its worst during the 1860s from every viewpoint. It had opposed the North during the American Civil War, it had cut its foreign and parliamentary services, and it was stuffed full of advertisements. When Scott took over as editor he was an incipient Liberal rather than the Radical he became. But from the very first, he showed his courage in espousing unpopular causes—and here let it be noted how curious it is that Manchester, whose prosperity was based on hard-headed, *laissez-faire* materialism, should be equally noted for a paper whose almost puritanical distaste, under Scott, for rampant commerce brought it constantly into collision with many of the city's leading business tycoons. For not every head of a Mancunian business firm was an Ernest Simon. Scott backed Irish Home Rule; he supported the striking dockers in 1889, the striking miners in 1893 and the striking engineers in 1897; he supported radical educational reforms; he opposed the Boer War, and his home and office were put under police protection. On the war issue, neighbours whose friendship he valued and work he admired broke off friendly relations with him and his paper.

Nor was he courageous only on matters of public importance. From 1895 to 1905 he was an M.P. and often left the paper to his trusted colleagues Montague (his son-in-law) and Hobhouse. But his cousin, Taylor, suspected him of neglecting his duties, and when Taylor's Will was published in 1905 it was found to contain a vaguely worded clause about the proprietorship which put Scott's and the paper's future in jeopardy. It is also probable that Taylor was deeply concerned about the effects of Scott's policies on the paper's finances. Though Scott had built circulation from 30,000 copies a day in 1880 to 48,800 in 1898 his Boer War stand began a decline to 36,000 by 1907, despite the Liberal victory of 1906. In the end Scott had to buy the paper's copyright, buildings and other assets at a full market price of £242,000. He did this by investing all his personal fortune of £48,000 as ordinary capital of a limited company. His relatives invested their capital too. For the rest of his life Scott never drew any interest and never paid himself a salary of more than £2,000 a year.

Scott, in fact, was a man of principle to an unyielding and magnificent degree, and, as Kingsley Martin has shrewdly written, he was also a fox as well as being a lion, a man to whom the adjective Macchiavellian could justly be applied. But he forgot that other men were frailer creatures, not all of them so completely bound up with their work and its ethics that considerations of private and personal gain melted away. To work for the *Guardian* was to become an acolyte to some religious calling— that was Scott's view. He underpaid his staff, not wilfully or neglectfully, but simply because he couldn't understand that anyone should fail to realise that the honour of working for a great newspaper overcame all material considerations. If someone left his employ, he was inclined to regard them as traitors and would dismiss them from his presence without a handshake and with little more than a formal word of farewell, if that. When Howard Spring left the *Guardian* for Beaverbrook's *Evening Standard* Scott's attitude was akin to that of a mother superior who has discovered that a novitiate was leaving the convent to take up employment in a brothel.

Other aspects of his work were flawed. One suspects that his strict adherence to a ban on racing news because of its association with betting was placation of his large Non-conformist readership rather than the reflection of intense personal feeling. "Comment is free, but facts are sacred" is Scott's most-quoted dictum: yet can this be squared with withholding news from the public because of a moral judgment? Another flaw was his occasional naïveté, shared by many of idealistically liberal outlook and best illustrated by his reaction in March 1917 to the news of the Russian Revolution:

> . . . a wonderful and glorious event. I've telegraphed the salutation of the *Manchester Guardian* editor and staff to the President of the Duma. . . . Don't you feel the Russian Revolution rather stirring in your bones, and making the growing invasion of personal liberty here more intolerable?

He was genuinely amazed when some of his friends felt unable to share his transports of delight.

No full corrective has yet been published—except in some books of memoirs—to two popular misconceptions about this great man and journalist. Puritanical as he may have seemed, austere and forbidding as are the almost fanatical eyes—the eyes of the champion of the oppressed minority everywhere—that pierce the observer of Epstein's marvellous portrait-bust, C. P. Scott was evidently a delightful man. People who knew him outside the office speak always of his charm and courtesy, his devastating good looks, his laughter. He was no ascetic about life. He enjoyed champagne, he liked gaudy flowers, he liked good glass, china, furniture and jewellery. He was an optimist, and believed that "somehow good will be the final goal of ill" provided one never gave up hoping and working.

In old age he mellowed in the office, and the best story about him that I know is not the too-often-told one of his nocturnal bicycle ride but of the occasion when, as a very old man, he asked Malcolm Muggeridge to write a short disparaging leader about a hideous gas holder which had recently been erected in the city. But it did not appear in the paper because someone had remembered that on that day there was also an advertising supplement for the gas company. Muggeridge received an explanatory note from Scott which contained the immortal sentence: "There are occasions on which truth should be economised in order not to make a hard task harder." Truth should be economised . . .! (Muggeridge wrote a novel about Manchester and the *Guardian* which was deemed too libellous for publication. Would it still be so regarded today?)

The other misrepresentation of Scott is journalistic. He is depicted as a kind of lofty all-father, dedicated to one thing and one thing alone: the long leader, a piece of holy writ, the soul of the paper etc. etc. Scott rightly attached prime importance to the leader, especially when he was writing it, but no editor ever built up a paper as Scott did on the leader alone. We do Scott less than justice if we forget that he was a superb newspaperman and that his entitlement to be considered a great editor is not a political judgment but is based on sheer professionalism. A. P. Ryan recounted once in a broadcast that he asked Scott's opinion on the reasons for the failure of *Tribune*, a Liberal daily started in Fleet Street in Edwardian times. The reply was revealing: "Those in charge concentrated on their leading articles and did not keep the news under hourly editorial control." It is fashionable to write of Scott's *Guardian* as though it were merely a symposium of articles on the erudite subjects of the day, a dilettante's intellectual feast. If you go through its files, you will find that it was crammed with news.

Scott was succeeded by his youngest son Ted, who was tragically drowned in Windermere three months after his father's death. (C.P. died sixty years to the day after he first occupied the editor's chair. Kingsley Martin considered that he stayed on too long, that although Ted had much of the actual responsibility for the paper in C.P.'s last years he still had to consult his father on almost everything.) W. P. Crozier took over after Ted Scott, and it was to his credit that the paper has such an honourable record in its attitude to the rise of Hitler. Its greatest editor since Scott—possibly, indeed, its greatest editor—was, however, A. P. Wadsworth, a strange unpredictable man, maddeningly indecisive yet with a very clear idea of where he and the paper were going. He was the last editor in the Scott tradition, the last individual sphere of influence in Manchester itself, yet unassuming and modest to the degree that for two years he refused to move into Scott's old room, preferring to remain in his own. Wadsworth died prematurely, being succeeded by Alastair Hetherington, a Scotsman then in his thirties. With Scott's grandson Laurence, Hetherington took major decisions to alter the outlook of the paper. He removed the word 'Manchester' from the title, a deed for which some Mancunians can still not find it in their hearts to forgive him, and he removed his chair to London, where the paper began to print.

It is too early to comment on the effects of these decisions on the history of the *Guardian*—and it is hardly the place of a journalist from another newspaper to probe into the intimate life of a rival—but it may still be said that the loosening of the *Guardian*'s ties with Manchester is as symbolic as the decline of the textile industry of the end of one phase of Manchester's modern history. The paper's circulation, however, has continued to rise.

Hetherington has not lacked any of Scott's dissenting fervour. Within days, almost, of his accession to the chair, he opposed the Suez adventure with as much ferocity as C. P. Scott had opposed the Boer War, and later still he broke with a *Guardian* tradition of identification with the Zionist cause by a friendly attitude towards the Arabs which enraged many of his Jewish readers. People could be heard saying "C. P. Scott would turn in his grave," but those who said it can have studied Scott's career very superficially, if at all. I have not the slightest doubt that he would have approved all the political stands taken by his present-day successor. He had foreseen as early as 1913 that the radical future lay with Labour.

That he would have disapproved of the change in the paper's title and the removal of its centre of gravity from Manchester to London is equally certain. He believed that everything Mancunian was superior; he loved the city and wanted to keep his staff in it where they could not be 'contaminated' by London's hot-house gossip. But if he were to come back and read his paper today, once he had recovered from the shock of adjusting himself to forty years of changes in outlook, prose and presentation, once he had accustomed himself to the outspoken women's page which deals unmistakably with women's topics, he would recognise that his work had not been in vain. It is still a writer's paper, still "a mosaic of brightly vari-coloured pieces", as Montague described it. It is still a paper that tries to make Manchester's businessmen think twice; still a champion of the minority; still idealistic, naïve, muddle-headed, right, wrong, infuriating and witty. And still indispensable, damn it!

TEN

PANORAMA

Scott lived in Fallowfield at 'The Firs', a long, low, elegant house built as the country villa of the engineer and inventor Sir Joseph Whitworth and said to have been designed by Edward Walters. When Whitworth died in 1887 he left the freehold of the building and the land to the trustees of the university, but Scott had lived in the house since 1881, and it was leased to him by the university. Some of the grounds became playing-fields. Now the house is the residence of the Vice-Chancellor. It had lost its rural isolation in Scott's time; today it is near the university settlement known as Owens Park. All this is very suitable and apposite, for Scott's ties with the university were close and nothing would have pleased him more than its enormous expansion in recent years. Some details of that expansion will be included in my last chapter. The university has been fortunate in its Vice-Chancellors, from the days of Sir Adolphus Ward and of Sir Alfred Hopkinson, who controlled its destinies at the time it achieved 'independence' from federal status. They would hardly envy the present, recently installed incumbent, Arthur Armitage, who has taken over at perhaps the most crucial time in the university's existence, when not only is the physical shape of the university changing and growing but the students are demanding a voice in the running of its affairs.

Mr. Armitage follows the tradition of his two great predecessors in being a Lancastrian. The Vice-Chancellor from 1934 until 1956 was Sir John Stopford—christened John Sebastian Bach Stopford by his father, a music-loving colliery engineer—later Lord Stopford of Fallowfield but known to everyone as 'Stoppie'—and known to everyone is no idle phrase, for it is said that he knew everyone in the university, from staff to cleaners. Stopford was a surgeon, and was Professor of Anatomy at Manchester when he was 31, succeeding Sir Grafton Elliot Smith. He made a close study of First World War cases and did his finest work on investigating the blood supply of the brain stem and on the neurological aspects of damage to the nerves of wounded soldiers. His appointment to the Vice-Chancellorship was a blow to medical science, but a gain to the academic world. He took the university through the war and presided over the difficult post-war years when austerity threatened growth at a time of a vastly increased student entry and the clamour for still more university places. But perhaps his greatest service was in his judgment of men to fill high academic posts—aided by his phenomenal powers as a diagnostician, which enabled him to eliminate some candidates on medical grounds on sight! He brought to Manchester Blackett and Hartree in physics, Wood Jones in anatomy, Manson in biblical studies, Willis Jackson in electro-technics, Rowley in Semitic languages, Goldstein in mathematics. He took special pride in the medical school and in the creation of full-time clinical chairs of medicine and neuro-logical and orthopaedic surgery, which were first filled by those legendary Mancunian medical men Robert Platt, Geoffrey Jefferson and Harry Platt.

When the National Health Service was founded in 1948, Jock Stopford became first chairman of Manchester Regional Hospital Board and undertook the daunting task of reforming the whole hospital system within the area. Although already a sick man, he entered with passion into these duties and his sincerity and zeal overcame much of the resentment at the revolutionary changes. He was a friendly man but a strong one. He loved his garden and football. He hated pretentiousness and he cut through it: serious-minded students who professed that they never listened to any-thing less elevated than Bach or read anything lighter than Tolstoy and Shakespeare would be told: "I simply don't believe you read Tolstoy in bed at night," (why not, by the way) and the barriers would come down.

To follow such a man is never an easy task; just as A. P. Wadsworth felt himself unworthy to sit in the chair of Scott and Crozier, so—and with equally little justification—William Mansfield Cooper considered that he was merely the follower of a great man. Yet almost more than Stopford he personified the Manchester University ideal. He was born in Newton Heath in 1903 and educated at an elementary school. At 14 he worked in a Denton hat factory, running messages for 6s. a week, and going to night school after the day's work was over. He studied book-keeping and shorthand, and in a year he changed jobs, becoming a clerk with a firm of accountants.

At this time he thought of journalism, and a brilliant journalist he could have become. (His youth oddly parallels that of Neville Cardus.) Not until he was 28 did he begin his academic career, when, after years of studies on Workers' Educational Association courses, he won a scholarship to Ruskin College. There he took a diploma in economic and political sciences and in 1933 took a three-year course in law at Manchester University, to which he returned as an assistant lecturer in 1938. He was called to the Bar in 1940 but never practised. The rest of his life was tied to Manchester University. He became Professor of Industrial and Commercial Law in 1949, he was Registrar and twice he acted as Vice-Chancellor when Stopford was ill. In 1956 he succeeded to Sir John's post and presided over the immense job of planning the university of tomorrow.

Small, neat, approachable, shrewd, warm-hearted, a lover of Manchester and Lancashire, of music and flowers, of books and of his fellow human beings, he was probably always happier as a teacher than as an administrator. He likes students and sympathises with their causes; it was ironic that his last two or three years as head of his own university were marred by manifestations of student unrest. However much he might have sympathised with some of their views, he certainly did not condone their methods of expressing them. Yet his whole life is a pattern to them of what application can achieve: no lavish council grants to help the Carduses and Mansfield Coopers of Edwardian Manchester.

The university has largely remained a research foundation, which is why its scientific and medical schools have won such repute. One would expect science to flourish in an industrial region, and from its foundation the Literary and Philosophical Society was concerned to promote links between the scientists of all nations. John Dalton's arrival in the city in 1793 and his consequent fifty years' membership of the 'Lit. and Phil.' gave the city its first international scientific lustre. His most notable pupil was J. P.

Joule, son of a Salford brewer, who conducted all his experiments with electro-magnetism in his laboratory between 1839 and 1871. Joule was never connected with Owens College, which, from its foundation in 1851, laid stress on its chemistry school. The creation of a thriving research school was the work of Henry Roscoe, who occupied the chair of chemistry for twenty-nine years, until 1886. Physics, too, was developed principally by Balfour Stewart, among whose pupils in Manchester was J. J. Thomson, discoverer of the electron. Yet Stewart's successor, Arthur Schuster, came near to that discovery in his work on cathode rays. Schuster supervised the construction of a new laboratory—known now as the Schuster Building—and voluntarily retired at the age of 56 on condition that he should be followed in the Chair by Ernest Rutherford. So from 1907–1919 Manchester's physics was headed by one whom many rank as the greatest physicist of all. Working with him to produce the science of nuclear physics were Ernest Marsden, James Chadwick, Charles Darwin, Niels Böhr and E. N. da C. Andrade. Their work culminated in 1919 with Rutherford's discovery of the first artificial nuclear disintegration—and, as Lady Bracknell observed on another occasion, "we all know what that unfortunate event led to". His successors in the Langworthy Chair have included Lord Blackett and Sir Brian Flowers, two nuclear physicists of the utmost distinction.

Nor should it be forgotten that Chaim Weizmann was a reader in biology at the University during the 1914–18 war and took to his friend C. P. Scott not only his views on Zionism but his plan for manufacturing chemicals for munitions. It was Scott who urged consideration of Weizmann's work on Lloyd George with such important results for the British war effort.

Today chemicals and plastics, encouraged by the oil industry, have become one of the major factors in Manchester's industrial growth. At Carrington, on the fringe of the city, Shell's huge petrochemical plant, with its lurid flares and curious space-age nocturnal picture of steam and energy, is one of the country's biggest expanding investments, linked by a 23-mile pipeline to the company's refinery and plant at Stanlow on the Dee Estuary. Imperial Chemical Industries are spread around the Manchester area, concentrating their dyestuffs and chemicals division on Blackley, where as long ago as 1865 there was a plant producing sulphuric acid and napthalene. But engineering and heavy industry are now the Manchester area's main source of wealth and employment. The A.E.I. group in Trafford Park alone employ nearly 17,000 workers. Ferranti in electronics, Hawker Siddeley in aircraft, are specialist employers. The number of smaller companies manufacturing machine tools and electrical components is legion. It is a long haul from the heyday of 1913 when cotton was all-powerful and Portland Street smelt of grey cloth.

One of the only major industries in which Manchester has no share is the motor-car. Yet before 1914, with Belsize and Crossley cars made at Clayton and Openshaw, Henry Royce building Rolls-Royce in the city, and Ford with a works in Trafford Park, it seemed as if Manchester might rival Coventry. But Ford went to Dagenham in 1929, Rolls-Royce went to Derby. Manchester's chief share in the car industry thereafter was selling them, and in 1945 James Agate observed of Deansgate that it seemed to be "entirely given over to motor-car salesmen". The great names associated with engineering in Manchester are William Fairbairn, whose work on the durability of cast-iron—early studies into 'metal fatigue'—was ahead of its time; and Joseph Whitworth, inventor of the screw-thread and a pioneer of precision measurement. He has been well called the 'father' of modern mass production; he also gave Manchester in 1842 its first road-sweeping machine, which helped to clean the city at a time when it badly needed it.

Manchester's reputation in medicine is the equal of Edinburgh's. Research and teaching have been its main concern, from the days of Charles White, towards the end of the eighteenth century, who recognised the infectious nature of puerperal fever and the need for cleanliness. Scientific study of medicine was introduced to Manchester by Sir William Roberts (1830–99), an expert on digestion and diet and part-time professor of medicine at the university in the 1870s and 1880s. Among his successors was Graham Steell, one of the first men to describe 'heart murmurs'. The city's great surgeons have included Walter Whitehead; E. D. Telford, who worked with Stopford on the nervous control of blood vessels; J. B. Macalpine, who drew attention to the serious industrial disease of cancer of the bladder in men engaged on making aniline dyes; Wilson Hey; W. R. Douglas; John Morley; Sir Harry Platt and Frank Nicholson. Yet perhaps Manchester medicine is most famous for its neurologists and neuro-surgeons. Stopford and Telford have been mentioned; James Ross, Sir William Thorburn and R. T. Williamson were names to conjure with in the nineteenth and early twentieth centuries. Outstanding, however, was Sir Geoffrey Jefferson, who died in 1961, and was probably the most widely known and frequently honoured of Manchester doctors. A physician before anything else, his clinical investigations into the possibilities of neuro-surgery had a profound influence on this branch of medicine, and it was said of him that if you mentioned his name in foreign medical circles, men crossed themselves! It may be a long time before the city again produces, as it has done recently, a president of each of the Royal Colleges—Sir Robert (now Lord) Platt (Physicians), Sir Harry Platt (Surgeons) and Sir William Fletcher Shaw (Obstetricians and Gynaecologists).

If Manchester is a good place in which to fall ill, it is also a good place in which to go to school. The foundation of the Free Grammar School by Hugh Oldham in 1515 has been mentioned in an earlier chapter. Although the income from the mills on the Irk ensured the school's prosperity, it was a mixed blessing. The school authorities were in fact running two businesses, one commercial and one educational. Moreover they had a monopoly. This led to ill feeling between 'town and gown' because, with the increase in population, the mills could not grind enough corn. Other mills were built, but these represented illegal competition for the Lord of the Manor and the school felt impelled to suppress them. In 1759 Parliament abolished the monopoly in grain and the school trustees now had to compete on the open market.

Towards the end of the eighteenth century the school's profits from grinding were substantial, but during the next century matters worsened until for five years the mill ran at a loss, and the revenue from malt diminished because brewers moved outside the town limits to escape the malt monopoly which Parliament had retained to the school. Salvation came with the railways, who not only put up a station next to the school in Long Millgate but bought all the mill land. Henceforward the income came not from flower but from chief rents. Also the railways brought pupils from all parts of Lancashire and Cheshire almost to the school gates.

Although Hugh Oldham's original humanitarian ideals had

been observed and the school remained free and open to all, nevertheless successive High Masters had enlarged the income by taking boarders. In the second half of the eighteenth century the grammar school was primarily for the sons of the gentry, and by 1825 its income was £4,000 a year, a very considerable sum. In 1833 the trustees obtained a court order giving them authority to use half their surplus to build a boarding house. But they had chosen the wrong moment. Already Manchester was growing conscience-stricken about its working-class's living conditions. Litigation to revoke the order followed and was successful. That was the end of the plan to create a boarding school in Manchester.

Thirty years later, however, in 1867, a scheme for the admission of fee-paying day boys was allowed, despite strong opposition. It was no longer the Free Grammar School. At first there were nine fee-payers. In 1883 there were 796. Today there are more than 1,400 pupils and the fees are £177 a year.

With almost monotonous regularity M.G.S. annually heads the list of scholarship winners to Oxford and Cambridge. Sheer weight of numbers, say the detractors, but they are on tricky ground: quantity does not necessarily ensure quality. In any case the tradition is not of recent birth. It stems from the efforts of the great F. W. Walker, appointed High Master in 1859 at the age of 27. (Incidentally, why is it thought that youth at the helm is a twentieth-century innovation? Take Victorian Manchester alone: Walker High Master at 27, Scott editor at 25, Hallé in charge of the Gentlemen's Concerts at 29.) Taking over at a time when the school was ailing financially and academically, he aimed for the stars. In those days the Oxford Local Examination, forerunner of the G.C.E., was the goal. Of 800 grammar schools in Britain only 230 put forward candidates, two or three boys each. Walker put forward forty a year. In 1863 every one of the dozen boys in his Classical Sixth was elected to an open scholarship or exhibition at Oxford or Cambridge. In his eighteen years in office, before he left to become High Master of St. Paul's School, he rebuilt the school (Waterhouse was the architect), quadrupled its numbers, raised £150,000, completely reorganised the curriculum and made it the great school it has remained.

Criticisms that M.G.S. is a brain-factory are forcefully rebutted by Mancunians. In one decade not long ago when 350 boys gained open awards at Oxford or Cambridge, 103 received Blues of one sort or another. The amount of non-scholastic activities is astonishing in its range and variety, and great importance is laid on it. There is no exceptional emphasis on specialisation, such as would justify the jibe 'swot shop', even in the Sixth, and school hours are shorter than in many other schools because of the distances many boys have to travel. The present High Master, Peter Mason, has said that "the boys themselves set the pace. They are intolerant of the second-rate." A recent edition of *Who's Who* contained nearly 200 Old Mancunians, among them politicians, journalists, barristers, industrialists, clergymen and the virtuoso pianist John Ogdon. Presumably none of them emulated Thomas de Quincey, who ran away in 1802.

Since 1931 the school has occupied buildings in 30 acres of playing fields in Fallowfield. The old buildings near the Irk had for long been overcrowded, insanitary and pervaded by the stench from the river. Yet even in such unsatisfactory conditions standards were maintained, thanks to the twenty-one-year High Mastership of J. L. Paton from 1903-24, and the equally long spell of D. G. Miller, who supervised the move to Fallowfield. He was followed in 1945 by Eric James (now Lord James of Rusholme), one of whose remarks is specially apt: "When I look through my study window I have no idea if the boy dropping an ice-cream paper is the son of an unemployed steel worker or comes from a home where the income runs into four figures." Local education authorities pay fees for about 65 per cent of the pupils; the remainder can claim part or total exemption from paying fees if parental income is small. This, Mr. Mason says, makes M.G.S. a truly comprehensive school socially.

The common denominator is exceptional ability, and the school ensures that it takes only the cream from its large catchment area by having its own tough entrance examination. Yet, under the Socialists, M.G.S. was uncertain of its fate as more local authorities became 'comprehensive'. The threat posed to direct grant schools such as M.G.S. by the withdrawal of grants by local education committees has never been underestimated by Mr. Mason, nor does he lie down under it. The cost to the Government of subsidising education in M.G.S. was about £62 a boy, considerably less than the cost of maintaining a boy at a comprehensive school, because neither fees nor grants contributed anything to capital costs.

With the Public Schools Commission's recommendation that all direct grant schools should 'go comprehensive', the probability was that M.G.S. would declare itself independent and the Manchester public school which failed to materialise in 1833 would be brought about by the pressures of the Welfare State. As Mr. Mason has said: "Is this for some people a consummation only less devoutly to be wished than the abolition of freedom to buy education at all, or is it just one more proof that nothing but nonsense can result from so prejudiced an inquiry? The cost in time, money and real progress and unpolitical goodwill is awful to contemplate." For the time being, the threat has receded.

What the parents and boys think of M.G.S. has been well demonstrated by the success of the £500,000 capital building fund appeal launched in 1968 for new buildings and modernisation of existing ones. Within four months over half had been collected. The boys themselves organised sponsored walks (guarantors offered anything from 1d. to £5 a mile). Industry and commerce gave £107,000, and the school was fortunate enough to have among its old boys five directors of Marks and Spencer Ltd., including Lord Sieff. Whatever the future may hold, anything that lowers the school's prestige and standards will not quickly or easily be forgiven the perpetrators.

But Manchester has another old, famous and picturesque school, Chetham's Hospital, which stands near the cathedral on the site it has occupied since its dedication in 1656. The buildings have been there longer and are, with the cathedral, the city's last sizeable medieval relic. They were erected between 1421 and 1446 when the church became collegiate under licence from Henry V (see Chapter 2), and Thomas La Warr rebuilt his baronial hall on a collegiate plan. During many vicissitudes as a result of religious strife, the college buildings passed in 1549 into the hands of the Stanley family, Earls of Derby.

In 1649 an approach to buy them was made by Humphrey Chetham, a bachelor who made a fortune from textiles and as a financier. He decided to dispose of his wealth by founding a school for poor boys, and for several years before his death in 1653 he had maintained twenty-two boys. His own approach to Lord Derby to provide a college for them failed but negotiations

The Piccadilly Plaza

were concluded in 1654 by the 'feoffees' appointed under his will. He left £7,000 to endow the school for forty pupils and left orders that the scholars "shall bee children of honest, industrious and painfull parents and not of wandering or idle beggars or roages nor that any of the said boyes shal bee basterds norr such as are lame, infirme or diseased att the time of their ellection". At the age of 14 the boys were to be "putt forth apprentice to some honest masters". The headmaster was (and still is) designated House Governor, and on the day of dedication it was declared that the school "fytly and justly be named by noe other name than by the name of Mr. Cheetham's Hospitall". The boys—numbering over 280 today—still (on some special occasions) wear, like their fellows at Christ's Hospital, blue coats and yellow stockings, and they also preserve the broad 'pancake' caps which Christ's abandoned. The boy boarders sleep under the noble timber roof of the Hospitium. They dine in the baronial hall, one of the finest fifteenth-century examples in existence, with its wide wood cove projecting over the dais and the two massive oak screens, or 'speers', projecting from the walls (originally to check draughts). A double-storeyed cloister ranges round three sides of the charming cobbled court. There must be hundreds of Manchester folk working and walking daily in this busy part of the city who do not even know that this magnificently preserved architectural treasure is in their midst.

The school faced its problems after the 1939–45 war with realism. The value of the endowments had dropped and the 'feoffees' incorporated those of Nicholls Hospital, a similar foundation, to form one independent grammar school taking more pupils, some of whom would pay. This was in 1952, and two years later the school appealed for £75,000 for new classrooms and laboratories which were opened in November 1955, appropriately enough by Lord Derby.

In 1969 Chetham's took an even bolder and more adventurous step. It has always had a fine musical tradition which was strongly developed after 1949 by the cathedral organist, Norman Cocker, who arranged for Chetham's to serve as a choir school for the cathedral and for the cathedral to provide exhibition scholarships for the choristers. He also formed a school orchestra, and the splendid work he did was carried on by his great friend, pupil and successor as director of the school's music, Gerald Littlewood.

Elisabeth Frink's "Flight" in Ringway concourse

Jodrell Bank, technology in a Cheshire field

But whereas many schools have musical activities, none of such a size had, before Chetham's, become a junior school of music. Yet Harry Vickers, the House Governor since 1949, decided on this bold step as a logical consequence of the growing numbers of musically-inclined entrants and in view of the establishment in the city of the new and splendidly equipped Northern College of Music. At the same time it was decided to admit girls, and the first thirty, of whom fourteen were boarders, joined in September 1969. From that date prospective pupils were examined musically only, but it was emphasised that general education would not suffer.

The eventual aim is for 200 boarders (eighty girls) and 150 day pupils. Boarding fees of £510 a year in 1969 were increased by £100, and many local authorities in the area agreed to support children at the school. For years musical educationists have deplored the late start to specialist training in Britain; at Chetham's children of 6 will be accepted if they show sufficient promise. The school has bought a large adjacent building to provide extra classrooms and dormitories for the girls. It has launched an appeal for a sum of £800,000 during the 1970s to pay for further expansion and accommodation. It aims to make the area round the cathedral as attractive as it must have been 400 years ago. This, surely, is the same bold spirit as Victorian Manchester showed.

Nor, while considering Chetham's, must one forget its famous and valuable library, claimed as the earliest free public library in Europe and packed with rare and beautiful books.

There are many other famous schools in Manchester, notable among them the William Hulme Grammar School and the Manchester High School for Girls at Fallowfield, both endowed by the Hulme Trust in 1881 and 1874 respectively. There are also the primary and comprehensive schools run by the education committee of the city council. The problem has always been that building has never caught up with the increasing numbers of children needing school places. As long ago as 1918 the city's distinguished director of education, Spurley Hey, said that Manchester needed "a continuous and almost unlimited supply of bricks and mortar for the next forty years".

Years ago the religious controversy dominated educational debates and reforms in the city—Cobden once said that repealing the Corn Laws was "light entertainment" compared with persuading priests of all denominations "to agree to suffer the people to be educated"—and in our time, and still continuing, the major educational controversy is between comprehensive education and the direct-grant, fee-paying schools. It is remarkable that Manchester has produced two women as the outstanding educational controversialists of their day. Lady Simon's rôle has already been discussed. If she enraged the Right Wing, they had their revenge with Kathleen Ollerenshaw, who has been the object of as much derision and as many vendettas as her older rival.

Born in Didsbury, a member of the Timpson family, brilliant mathematician (but bad speller), a graduate of Somerville and later an Oxford don, Lancashire hockey-player, wife of a distinguished surgeon, Dr. Ollerenshaw believes that comprehensive schools and direct-grant schools can and should co-exist. Her doctrine is that "if a large city like Manchester cannot accept variety in its education system, then things in this country will have come to a pretty pass". Thousands of parents are glad that she is in a position to ensure that her views prevail, but she would be the last person to underestimate the strength of the opposition.

Educationists hold the nation's future in their care, yet there are two other elements in the panorama of Manchester which have influenced its history as much as any schooling: water and smoke. By water I do not mean the rain which has kept comedians in business for so long, but the water supply. The visitor from the South when he first visits Manchester and goes to wash his hands is amazed by the amount of lather that comes from the soap. There is no 'fur' in the kettles boiled in Manchester, for the 'soft' water has none of the properties which cause it. This water comes direct from the Lake District, and it has caused in its time as much controversy as any educational programme. The proposal in the 1950s to eliminate the city's financial aid to its famous orchestra did not bring such widespread and universal derision upon the city as did 'the Ullswater affair' in 1961–2.

Manchester first took water from Thirlmere in 1894 and from Haweswater in 1919. It became impossible for the public to gain access to the shores of these lakes. Thirlmere is surrounded by a wall and fencing. Gates are locked and notices say "Trespassers will be prosecuted". The levels of the lakes were raised when they became reservoirs; the village of Mardale and surrounding land were 'drowned' to increase the size of Haweswater. So when Manchester Waterworks Committee, realising that the future needs of the city's industry and inhabitants could not be met in the 1970s if a new source was not tapped, proposed in 1961 to promote a parliamentary bill to build a reservoir in the Bannisdale Valley and to build a weir at the head of Ullswater there was a national outcry.

No one denied Manchester's needs. Residents of the city in the 1950s will remember the irony of driving into town in the rain, perhaps after a match at Old Trafford had been abandoned, to be accosted by a large poster depicting an Arab who told us: "If you lived in my country you would save water." It invited graffiti and got them. What was seriously questioned by the less hysterical sections of the opposition was whether the alternative sources of supply had been examined, or was Manchester going for the cheapest and easiest way? It was also generally felt that there had been something secretive about the way Manchester went about its new plan. Lakeland farmers, so they said, awoke to find corporation engineers and geologists drilling on their land. Why couldn't they have asked permission first; and anyway, why couldn't they invest in sea desalination schemes?

The issue, which perhaps could profitably have opened up the wider question of a national water policy, became a straight fight between wicked Manchester, the ugly grabbing marauder, and fair Ullswater, which was to be despoiled, raped, murdered and just wanted to be left alone with its thousands of tourists. It was fought in the House of Lords on 8th February 1962 in a superb debate. The opposition to Manchester was led by a son of the Lake District, Ulverston-born Lord Birkett, great advocate in many a murder trial and now defending his native heath in the beautiful voice and elegant language that had beguiled juries. His speech persuaded their Lordships to delete the Ullswater and Bannisdale clauses from the Bill by seventy votes to thirty-six. On the morrow of his victory, when flags were flown throughout the Lake District, he died.

But although Manchester had been told, in effect, to jump into the lake, it did not abandon its convictions. Metropolitan juris-diction of the kind meted out by the Lords had never been appreciated in Manchester, which saw itself once again as the victim of meddling by Whitehall bureaucrats in matters of which they had little practical knowledge. Further talks were held and a new plan was produced for taking 45 million gallons a day from Ullswater and Windermere. Manchester gave assurances that there would be no harm to the area's natural beauty, nor interference with public use and enjoyment of the Lakes' amenities and surroundings. Opposition was again strong, but not this time so fierce. In 1966 the Labour Government approved the new plans under certain conditions designed to counteract some of the fears of the scheme's critics, and even they are now full of praise for the care taken by the engineers to ensure that, once the work is completed and water is taken from Ullswater in 1971, all sign of the pumping equipment will be invisible. This has added £250,000 to the cost of the operation.

Clean soft water is one thing; dirty air quite another. Descriptions have been given in an earlier chapter of the pall of smoke that hung over Manchester for well over a century, blackened its buildings and did heaven knows what damage to the lungs of its inhabitants. Manchester was very slow to do anything about its smoke—no doubt, the cynics would say, because although smoke meant dirt and disease it also meant money and trade.

Some efforts to control the emission from chimneys were made in the 1840s, but John Bright, to his shame, and other 'chimney owners' of the North had the smoke clause taken out of the 1848 Public Health Act. It was another eighteen years before action could be taken against factory owners whose chimneys could be "deemed to be a nuisance" (masterly understatement). For the next half-century Manchester put out a great deal of propaganda against smoke, but did very little about it until, in 1924, it took the lead in forming a smoke abatement committee representing fifty-six local authorities in the region.

This did what it could but it was always realised that the only real answer was not merely to control the smoke but to do away with it altogether. This policy, based on the creation of smokeless zones, was formulated in the 1930s by Charles Gandy, a president of the Manchester smoke abatement society.

After the 1939-45 war Manchester took steps effectively to eliminate industrial smoke, but domestic chimneys were a major contributory factor to air pollution. After long delays, during which Coventry went ahead to become the first city with a smokeless zone, Manchester on 1st May 1952 declared a 105-acre area of the central business area to be a smokeless zone. Only smokeless fuels could be burned in the grates. Nearly twenty years later smokeless zones and smoke control areas cover 13,000 acres and 80,500 premises, and more zones are constantly being created and would be created quicker if the fuel industry was not in such a mess.

The effect is easy to see. Fogs are less frequent and less sulphurous. Buildings which have been cleaned have stayed clean. Bronchitis and catarrh, though still prevalent, have decreased. The sheep on the hills outside the city look whiter. A friend who returned by air from the United States recently said to me: "You have no idea what a thrill it was, after flying over the gloomy American cities, to see Manchester gleaming white below me. Manchester is a clean city now."

And now, I suppose, having avoided it long enough, I must, to conclude this chapter, mention the weather. Protected by the Pennines to the east and open to the sea in the west, Lancashire has on the whole a mild climate. Sheltered to north and east, Manchester rarely has a heavy snowfall. The smokeless zones have helped to increase the sunshine totals because the opacity of the urban atmosphere has been reduced.

Humidity in summer is high, and the rainfall in July and August, like that of half the British Isles, tends also to be high. But figures prove that Manchester is well down the 'league table' of rainy cities. When it does rain, however, it is rarely the torrential downpour of the south-west, but a slow steady rain or drizzle of longer duration. On such a day the notoriety Manchester has gained is understandable. But it is for most of the time an undeserved notoriety.

Legends die hard, however, and people will continue to believe that 'it's always raining in Manchester' whatever evidence is adduced to the contrary, just as they will continue to believe that it was the rain and humidity that led the cotton industry to develop in Lancashire, whereas the important factors were the soft water supply and the proximity of the coalfields. But legends are so much more attractive than the truth.

ELEVEN

GREATER MANCHESTER

THE great debate has begun that will affect the lives of millions of people in the Manchester area, yet you will hardly ever hear it discussed in clubs and pubs. For the man in the pub the principal topic is still the way City played on Saturday, or how limited the choice of beer is becoming. The rates? They are a necessary and unpleasant fact of life and the only thing to say about them is that they always seem to be going up. Yet in town halls and committee rooms, the topic that will be in foreground and background of meetings on all conceivable municipal topics during the next few years is the implementation or otherwise of the proposals contained in Lord Redcliffe-Maud's Royal Commission report on local government in England. Whatever happens to 'Maud', as it has become known, whether Mr. Heath consigns it to the shelf, like many another Royal Commission report, or whether it is whittled by governmental action to vanishing-point, nevertheless the ideas it contains have been 'kicked around' for some years now and they will form a continuing element in all discussions of reform of local government, whichever party is in power.

The eleven members of the Commission while by no means unanimous on many aspects of their conclusions were unanimous about one thing: that local government in England needs a new structure and a new map. Excluding London they proposed that there should be sixty-one new local government areas. For fifty-eight of these a single authority would be responsible for all services. But in the three metropolitan areas around Birmingham, Liverpool and Manchester they proposed that this responsibility should be divided between a metropolitan authority with planning, transport and major development under its aegis, and a number of metropolitan district authorities whose key functions would be education, social services (child care, welfare, care of the homeless, care of the handicapped, education welfare and child guidance, day nurseries, home help, mental health social work, adult training centres, etc.) health and housing. These sixty-one areas would be grouped, with Greater London, in eight provinces, each with its own council which would "settle the provincial strategy and planning framework within which the main authorities will operate". These provincial councils would replace the existing regional economic planning councils. And what would happen to the local councils we all have now? These would still be elected

> to represent and communicate the wishes of cities, towns and villages in all matters of special concern to the inhabitants. The only *duty* of the local council would be to represent local opinion, but it would have the *power* to do for the local community a number of things best done locally, including the opportunity to play a part in some of the main local government services on a scale appropriate to its resources and *subject to the agreement of the main authority*.

Those eight words are italicised by me, not by Lord Redcliffe-Maud, who does not tell us what will happen if the local council resolutely refuses to agree that the provincial council knows best what is right and proper for its little community. Somehow I do not think that his Lordship has attended many meetings of Lancashire local councils.

In considering the Manchester area—the SELNEC (South East Lancashire and North East Cheshire) conurbation—the Commission was motivated by population and housing considerations. The SELNEC metropolitan area becomes Unit 23 of the Northwest Province. It is perhaps important to record the Maud definition of this metropolitan area:

In terms of existing administrative areas it comprises Bolton, Bury, Manchester, Oldham, Rochdale, Salford, Stockport, Warrington and Wigan—all county boroughs.

In Cheshire it takes in:

(a) Altrincham, Dukinfield, Hyde, Macclesfield, Sale and Stalybridge—boroughs.
(b) Alderley Edge, Bollington, Bowdon, Bredbury and Romiley, Cheadle and Gatley, Hale, Hazel Grove and Bramhall,

Knutsford, Longdendale, Lymm, Marple, Middlewich, Northwich, Wilmslow and Winsford—urban districts.
(c) Bucklow, Disley, Macclesfield, Northwich, Tintwistle—rural districts.
Part of Runcorn rural district.

From Derbyshire are included:

(a) Glossop—borough.
(b) New Mills, Whaley Bridge—urban districts.
(c) Chapel-en-le-Frith rural district.

From Lancashire:

(a) Ashton-under-Lyne, Eccles, Farnworth, Heywood, Leigh, Middleton, Mossley, Prestwich, Radcliffe, Stretford, Swinton and Pendlebury—boroughs.
(b) A number of urban districts which include Atherton, Denton, Droylsden, Irlam, Turton, Westhoughton and Worsley.
(c) Warrington and Wigan rural districts.

From Yorkshire: Saddleworth urban district.

All this represents a vast and scattered area, nearly 1,050 square miles of it, with a present population of 3.2 million which by 1980 will certainly be nearer to 3.6 million. Of the nine metropolitan districts within SELNEC, Manchester is defined as Manchester and Salford, Ringway, and the boroughs and urban districts of Eccles, Prestwich, Stretford, Swinton and Pendlebury, Irlam and Urmston. Worsley goes into the Bolton district; Altrincham, Sale, Bowdon, Hale, Knutsford and Mobberley would become part of the Altrincham-Northwich district; Wilmslow and Alderley Edge would be in Stockport's area. The Commission names Manchester, Salford, Stretford and Urmston as the core of the whole conurbation, the aim being to keep the size of Manchester district to a minimum.

It was not difficult to guess what the reactions would be to this no doubt benevolent attempt to reorganise lives on doctrinaire socialist lines, creating bigger authorities in the time-honoured but practice-dishonoured belief that bigger means better, whereas experience has shown that it means cumbersome, remote and unfeeling. Cheshire and Lancashire County Councils, abolished by the giant Merseyside and Manchester metropolitan areas, determined to fight the proposals to the death. Typical of Lancashire local council reaction was that of the Mossley councillor who said: "We are being thrown to the wolves." A "nightmarish system", said the Lancashire County Council statement on the Commission's report, "complicated, confused and unworkable". The city of Manchester, of course, has long advocated the creation of a Greater Manchester Council giving a bigger rate catchment area and enabling it to improve many features of local life over which it has at present no control.

But local loyalties and traditions die hard. If logic says that Greater Manchester is a good administrative idea, local patriotism and pride are not so sure. Take as example the Westhoughton case in 1963. It began in 1958 when the council at Westhoughton, a town of 16,000 people near Bolton, voted by a narrow majority to let Manchester build over 12,000 houses in the town to accommodate over 42,000 'overspill' Mancunians. Immediately public opinion in the town rallied opposition to these proposals, the party which had approved the plan was thrown out at the next local election and the new council had second thoughts and opposed Manchester's 'land grab'. A long public inquiry into the scheme was held in the winter of 1963. Words like 'social apartheid' were used in evidence. The ill-feeling in the town was obvious from the heated language used. Prayers for the success of 'keeping out Manchester' were offered in a church and the clergyman's Christian principles were called into question. All in vain. A Conservative Government Minister ruled in favour of the new town plan. Then what happened? Talks on the overspill plan between Manchester and Westhoughton ran into troubled waters. Manchester accused Westhoughton of 'obstruction'. The change of government in 1964 had had its effect, and Manchester was told by Richard Crossman that it could only compulsorily purchase 1,906 of the 3,092 acres it had wanted at Westhoughton. The attitude of Westhoughton was uncompromisingly expressed by its council chairman: "If Manchester keeps on the right side of us and tries to see things our way, all well and good. If not, we are not going to be very co-operative." There could be only one outcome. In October 1966 the Ministry of Housing and Local Government withdrew support from the scheme because it could see no hope of reconciling the two antagonists; and Manchester

abandoned its plans. "We have had a bellyful," said one Mancunian alderman. "We have tried in every way possible to secure
a New Town development. In turn we have suggested Lymm,
Mobberley and Westhoughton and none has succeeded." All this,
and Ullswater too!

David had slain Goliath again and all the friends of the little
men threatened by powerful multi-corporations gave Westhoughton a cheer. But some of the little town's inhabitants had
their misgivings. After all, £50 million worth of Manchester
money had been turned away, and shopkeepers and businessmen
were not too pleased about that. "We've no dance hall, no
cinema, no bowling alley, nothing," said a Westhoughton youth.
The older people said: "We're all right left as we are." And on the
day of his victory the chairman of Westhoughton council said:
"Now we can get down to the business of running our town
again." If Lord Redcliffe-Maud had his way, Westhoughton
would be run as part of Unit 23(b), Bolton Metropolitan District
of the SELNEC Metropolitan Area, North-West Province.

Poor Manchester, it was the Great Unwanted in the 1960s. Its
rejection by Westhoughton is a more significant example of the
stubborn spirit of independence which exists in Lancashire than
the Ullswater affair. Ullswater is a long way from Manchester and
a beauty spot. Westhoughton is just up the road. It had no silver-
voiced Norman Birkett to speak for it, only the rough accents of
its inhabitants. But 'Keep out' has the same effect in any accent.
You would think, to read the yards of newspaper space devoted
to it between 1959 and 1966, that Westhoughton was engaged in
repelling a twentieth-century Babylon, perhaps even Sodom or
Gomorrah. Keep us, the argument ran, from contact with this
city which only wants to settle its slum families on us, this city
which is merely tacked on to the very tip of Lancashire, this city
full of Scotsmen and Yorkshiremen and Londoners, of actors and
journalists and students and TV folk. Perhaps they were right;
only time will tell. For me, Westhoughton is immortalised in one
of the best of Neville Cardus's Lancashire cricket stories. It has
appeared in print before, but it deserves repeating, anthologising
so to speak. It concerns burly Dick Tyldesley, the great bowler.
Lancashire were fielding and Tyldesley took a brilliant catch low
down. The batsman began his walk back to the pavilion but
Tyldesley waved him back. "It were not out," he told the

umpire—his hand had touched the ground. When stumps were drawn Cardus congratulated Tyldesley on his sportsmanship—no one would have been any the wiser if he had let the batsman continue on his way. "Ah well, Mester Cardus," Dick replied, "that's Westhoughton Sunda' school, tha knows."

What are they like, these towns that belong to the Greater Manchester concept and stand like sentinels around the city, thinning out as one goes north where industrial Lancashire (which is how most people think of that beautiful county) gives way to the loveliness of the Ribble Valley and the Trough of Bowland and all the historical towns and villages that surround Lancaster itself until the grandeur and peace of the Lake District are reached? Sentinels is perhaps a word they will accept; satellites, never. Oldham, Stockport, Bury, Bolton, Wigan, Rochdale: they have their own history and identity, but they are within the Manchester orbit. It is only in the west, when we reach Warrington, that we begin to feel the gravitational pull of the other rival giant, Liverpool. Yet 'Maud' has included Warrington in the SELNEC area, not the Merseyside district, because of the new town to be built at Risley on the Manchester side and largely to take people from Manchester. (Yes, a home for the overspill at long last, though not where Manchester really wanted it.) "This makes it probable", says the report, "that Warrington's links with the Manchester area will increase more than its links with Liverpool." At any rate these towns have their place in a portrait of Manchester: they are part of the background, and like the centrepiece of the portrait, they are all busily engaged in bulldozing away the past, superimposing a glass-and-concrete image of shiny brilliance on the grey, cobbled face presented for years past to wind and weather and the lenses of cameramen anxious to illustrate what Blake meant by dark, satanic mills, though in fact, of course, he did not mean the terraces and factories of Lancashire.

First there is the inner ring of towns that long ago surrendered their identity to Manchester, keeping their names but becoming postal districts. Perhaps that is unfair to Didsbury, Fallowfield, Withington, Chorlton-cum-Hardy, Stretford and Ardwick; after all, they retain individuality. But they would not deny that they are Manchester, by every kind of rating, just as Chelsea and Kensington are London. Not so Salford, Manchester's nearest neighbour, its twin, separated only by the Irwell but a city in its own right with quite a different atmosphere from Manchester which it regards as slightly parvenu and reprehensible. Salford, as readers will recall from an earlier chapter, is 'senior' to Manchester. Lord Redcliffe-Maud will have none of that sort of sentiment, of course. Good hard figures only suffice for him:

> The present boundary between Manchester and Salford county boroughs does not correspond to any physical, economic or social realities. . . . For its size Salford has very limited shopping importance (although there are schemes to improve it) but it contains the Manchester Ship Canal dock system and a great deal of associated warehousing and heavy industry. The strong economic inter-relationship between the two places is illustrated by the 1966 journey-to-work figures. No less than [he meant no fewer than] 31,200 of Salford's 69,100 economically active residents worked outside, in spite of Salford's big concentration of industrial employment. Of these, Manchester took 16,100, easily the largest single number. In the other direction 9,200 Manchester residents travelled to work in Salford.

Unanswerable, but I can think of some 'economically active residents' of Salford who would still point out Salford's claims to be regarded as a separate entity. For years its police force, now merged with Manchester's, set the pace for the rest of the country in pioneering new traffic-control methods; its collection of well over one hundred drawings and paintings by Lowry was valued at nearly £83,000 a few years ago and is assuredly worth much more already; its most famous recent inhabitant was John Barbirolli, who lived in an imposing house well surrounded by trees, a view, as he liked to point out, that could be in the depths of the countryside; its university, formerly the Royal College of Advanced Technology, is supplying industry with brilliant graduates. So it is hardly surprising that Salford's working party report on the Maud proposals rejected the idea of total merger with Manchester, adding that Manchester's preponderance "could be a source of stress and conflict". Despite the continuing fall in Salford's population it was, said its defenders, gaining in importance as an employment centre so that the number of its residents working in Manchester was declining.

It is Salford, of course, that Walter Greenwood used as the background of his classic novel of the 1930s depression *Love On The Dole* (are there many better titles?). 'Hanky Park' today has gone and in its place stand the high flats (Hankinson Street was its real name). Yet for everyone who remembers the significance of Hanky Park, tens of thousands today know another Salford street, also due for demolition, Archie Street. This is the street shown in the credit-titles of the television serial 'Coronation Street', thereby perpetuating a view of Salford as false and inaccurate as the interminable programme's depiction of Lancashire life. No one wanted to preserve Hankinson Street and Archie Street as pieces of industrial archaeology—comradeship in adversity was the only good thing that came out of them. But Salford has preserved an aspect of Victorian life which is a constant source of delight to visitors to the art gallery and museum at Peel Park. This is 'Larkhill Place', a Victorian street, with its shop windows displaying the wares of a century ago, a front parlour in all its homely comfort and warmth, kettle on the hob, cat sleeping by the fire, rocking-chair awaiting its next occupant. You can teach children more about life in the Great Queen's day by spending an hour in Larkhill Place than by any amount of textbook instruction.

Peel Park, named after Sir Robert, stands in The Crescent, the fine curving sweep of road which in Georgian times must have been one of the most desirable places for a residence in Lancashire, commanding a wonderful view. The museum and art gallery are due for eventual demolition and replacement, and Larkhill Place may then be moved to Ordsall Hall, which has been the subject of one of Salford's great post-war controversies. This hall was once the home of the Radclyffe family, one of whom is said to have bought the first Flemish weavers to England and settled them in Salford. Built in the fourteenth and sixteenth centuries, it has a magnificent example of a timber-roofed hall and a star chamber. Guy Fawkes is said to have hatched the Gunpowder Plot there— on the rather dubious evidence of the novelist Harrison Ainsworth. Once it was moated, but now it stands amid dockland, an extraordinary survivor into a very different Salford from the town John Radclyffe knew. In 1960 the hall was bought by Salford Corporation for use as a museum, but after £42,000 had been spent on restoring it from the depredations of vandals work was abandoned because the council could not face the prospect of £7,000 a year maintenance costs. But the council played their cards very cleverly. They tried to find a buyer and they also gave the Ministry of Housing six months' notice of their 'reluctant' intention to demolish the hall. Eventually a Government grant was forthcoming and Salford voted a further £7,500 to complete the restoration and to provide a local history and archaeology museum. Salford also wants to preserve its remarkable Gothic church of St. Paul's with Christ Church, built in 1856, by spending £38,000 on new foundations, floors, walls and redecoration. In its heyday this church, with its odd spire within a colonnade, had galleries round three sides, a large double-deck pulpit, and a domed sanctuary with three mosaic panels. It is as well worth preserving as the famous Flat Iron Market where jumble of an astonishing variety can be bought. Credit, too, to Salford for its decision to avoid building any more multi-storey flats. "We say, an end to the monstrosities of the concrete prisons which have been thrown up in this city to heights of 16, 17 and 23 storeys," was the finance committee's imperious declaration. "In future the limit will be five or six storeys."

Bolton is another town that said 'no' to overspill from Manchester. Going there from Manchester you pass through Moses Gate, a reminder of the deep religious strife which is part of Lancashire's history. Bolton is a sturdy place, a bastion of cotton but now the home of other industries; the home, too, of one of the finest series of chamber-music concerts to be found in the country and the home of one of the best modern theatres, the 'Octagon', opened in 1967 at a cost of £90,000. The 'Octagon' is a symbol of Bolton's enterprise and faith in its future and is worth detailed comment. But first what do Lord Redcliffe-Maud and his friends say about the Bolton metropolitan district of 86 square miles? Bolton, they write, "is a considerable industrial town and employment magnet. It is also a big shopping and commercial centre, providing a wide range of urban services, second in the metropolitan area only to Manchester. The Bolton district is a compact and natural unit of local government, with many links between the places included in it." In the prose of a Royal Commission, that ranks as a glowing tribute. The 'Octagon' is covered, presumably, by the phrase 'urban services'. For one thing, it is the first new theatre to be built in the North-west since the First World War. When the Second World War ended Bolton had four professional theatres but one by one they closed, the last of them, the 'Hippodrome', in 1960. Television and the cinema had beaten them; also the stars of the halls, artists like George Formby and Gracie Fields, had had their day. Part of Lancashire folklore was a night at the 'Hippodrome', be it in Bolton, Manchester, Ardwick or Salford, with the unforgettable Frank Randle getting away with murder in a way that must have made Max Miller green with envy—or perhaps blue with apoplexy would be an apter metaphor. At any rate, for seven years Bolton had no theatre but it had plans for an arts centre in the splendid town centre development opposite the imposing central library. The 'Octagon' was built there, right in the middle of the town. Its capacity is realistic, varying between 340 and 420 according to whether an 'open end' stage, or a 'thrust' stage, or theatre-in-the-round is in use. Its policy has so far been enterprising, supporting local playwrights such as Bill Naughton and Henry Livings, producing plays by Joe Orton and Peter Nicholls, and staging the classics too. Once a year it produces a documentary dealing with some aspect of the town's history, a rather unnecessary and artistically perilous ritual. The theatre also contains a drama workshop in a studio built and equipped by the Gulbenkian Foundation so that courses can be maintained all the year round for teachers, adults, youths and children.

The modern Bolton spirit was also shown in 1965 by its engagement of the architect Graeme Shankland to produce a comprehensive scheme for redevelopment of the town centre at a cost of £19 million. There was opposition, modification, a public inquiry, but the scheme will take shape. It was Bolton, too, that took immediate action to transform the Halliwell area of the town, described by a Government survey as a "typical twilight area" where little new had been built since 1890 and there were poor lay-out, few gardens, atmospheric pollution and general unsightliness. Clearing all this away and putting up new—that is the theme of Lancashire today.

When in 1967 textiles ceased to be the principal source of employment in Bolton, one of the town's officers described this as "an event of some historical significance". Manchester was the great market for cotton, the shop-window and commercial centre; it was in towns like Bolton and Oldham where the work was done, where the chimneys pointed grimly to the smoke-laden sky. Bolton is the town of Samuel Crompton, inventor of the spinning-mule. On the pedestal of his statue in Bolton he is shown

Medieval survivor, the Old Wellington Inn

sitting at the mule with a violin on the floor behind him: he used
to play it in a Bolton theatre. Crompton's memorial is, I suppose,
the prosperity and the squalor of nineteenth-century Lancashire,
but a more particular memorial is at the Tudor house of Hall-i'-
th'-Wood on the outskirts of Bolton, once the home of noble
families but even by the eighteenth century in poor repair, with
its rooms let as tenements to the poor for a few shillings a week.
It was in one of these rooms that Crompton lived, playing the
organ, singing the hymns he wrote and inventing the machine
which made other men a fortune but not him, for he was tricked
out of his rightful rewards. What he did, working at night in a
small attic for five years, was to combine Hargreaves's spinning-
jenny and Arkwright's frame and to improve on both. He
produced material of hitherto unimaginable fineness and delicacy,
and his fame spread. Manufacturers wanted machines like his and
a group of them signed a declaration promising him rich profits
if he gave them his secret. In fact he received £68. Poor Crompton applied to Parliament for recompense, and the Prime
Minister, Spencer Perceval, agreed to propose a grant of £20,000.
On the very night he was to do so he was murdered. Eventually
Crompton was given £5,000, which he promptly lost by unwise
investment. He died, a broken man, living on the charity of a few
friends.

Bolton's other hero comes from further back in history: the
seventh Earl of Derby, a title to which he succeeded while, as
Lord Strange, he was engaged in besieging Manchester on King
Charles I's behalf in 1642, as already related in Chapter 5. He
failed, for he was a home-loving, literary and religious man rather
than a soldier, with a French wife and devoted to his garden and
his home at Lathom. He did not lack courage and loyalty, and it
is said that it was he who guided Charles II to safety at Boscobel
after the Battle of Worcester in 1651. But he was captured and
condemned at Chester to death. He escaped from Chester Castle
by sliding down the walls on a rope, but again he was seized and
taken, on Cromwell's orders, to Bolton. But the Boltonians
would not build a scaffold for him, and his execution in the
market-place was delayed until one was ready. He asked for the
block to be moved so that he could see Bolton church and he had
twice to give the signal to the executioner that he was ready, so
unwilling was the man to carry out his duty on one who had just

Albert Square in the snow

said to him: 'Friend, be no more afraid to strike than I am to die'.

Bolton notwithstanding, the cotton town where King Cotton may be said to have had his throne was undoubtedly Oldham. In its heyday 145,000 men and women worked in its mills, 250 of them with 18 million spindles. Twice a week its dealers went to Manchester to join 10,000 others on the floor of the Royal Exchange, 10,000 dealers with control of 750,000 looms and over 50 million spindles. And today the Exchange has ceased to function. Oldham is on the eastern border of Lancashire with Yorkshire. Just beyond it the western slopes of the Pennines frown over the man-made scene. It is as if man and nature were in perpetual conflict to provide the most forbidding aspect. Here in Oldham you can still see in all their starkness the rows of identical houses, can imagine the knocker-up as he went his rounds summer and winter, can hear the clogs on the cobblestones as the mill-workers poured forth on their way to work. It is a haunted place. But it is changing. The bulldozers are at work there, too, the town map is being re-drawn. Let's hope the towns of the 1980s have as much character as they had in the 1880s. Mucky they may have been, but they had grandiose ideas. Bolton's municipal buildings are on an imposing scale. So are Oldham's, its town hall built like a Greek temple, with a pillared portico and a window in which Art, Industry, Commerce, Mechanism and Science are symbolised beneath the arms of Lancashire's manufacturing towns and Oldham's benefactors. Oldham's art gallery has long been notable among provincial galleries for the excellence of its collection, its fine watercolour section having developed from the nucleus of the gift of Charles Lees's collection towards the end of the nineteenth century. The Lees family have made money from Oldham but they have spent most of it on the town, and it is true to say that there would be no Royal Manchester College of Music had it not been for the generosity of this same Charles Lees. One of the first seventy-six students at that college in 1893 was a bass from Oldham named Charles Walton. Nine years later he had a son, William, today Sir William Walton O.M., one of Britain's great composers. There is no accounting for genius: it may arise from Stratford upon Avon as easily as from Bonn. But there is usually something in the environment that nurtures the seed. Mid-century Victorian Worcester may seem an unlikely milieu for Edward Elgar, but not when we remember the Three Choirs

Festivals, the local music societies, and his father's music shop in the High Street. Similarly in Walton's music, in the salvoes of brass in the First Symphony and *Belshazzar's Feast* and in the grand massed choral splendour of *Belshazzar's Feast* there is the Lancashire tradition of the brass bands and the oratorios. Bluff Oldham is not all that far away from the polished and sophisticated art of the composer of *Façade*.

Bury, home of the 'black pudding', is within the Manchester orbit and only nine miles from the city itself. 'Maud' groups it with Rochdale as a SELNEC metropolitan district, and notes that one of its neighbouring towns, Whitefield, is an important Manchester residential area. Neither Bury nor Rochdale, each of them as sturdily independent as any Lancashire towns you can find, views this grouping with much enthusiasm. Though John Kay, inventor of the shuttle, was one of Bury's two most famous sons—the other was Sir Robert Peel—it has never been merely a cotton town. Today its population is steadily increasing as it attracts more and more industries, 65,000 inhabitants in 1970 and a possible 85,000 ten years hence. Textiles, paper-making (one of the big industries of the North-west, incidentally), engineering, furniture, bedding, confectionery, paint, luggage, rubber, man-made fibres, footwear, plastics, oils, glues—name it, Bury makes it. It is not an old town. Its oldest building, a pub called the 'Two Tubs', is 1747. The town hall is 1954 and the parish church is 1870s, both magnificent of their period. I wish I could say the same for the main shopping street which has the splendidly unusual name The Rock and used to have some unusual lettering above the shops, some quaint doorways, a bit of character. Today it is just like any other suburban High Street, uniform, garish, a chain of chain stores. The new shopping precinct is like any other shopping precinct. The shoppers, many of them, come from the new housing estates which have taken the place of the derelict parts of the town. It's a dormitory town now—which certainly does not imply somnolence—and in its new rôle it is finding prosperity whatever price is paid in individuality. Is one just being a Lancashire sentimentalist to regret it? I don't suppose the survivors of the Depression do.

Another part of Lancashire history is enshrined in Bury. It was the depot town of the Lancashire Fusiliers, now part of the Regiment of Fusiliers. In the 1914–18 war seventeen members of this regiment won the Victoria Cross, and on a Sunday each April Bury still commemorates the deeds of the 1st Battalion at Gallipoli in 1915. The North-west is still the army's best recruiting area.

Rochdale, birthplace of John Bright, is one of the grandest Lancashire towns, grand in its history and outlook, grand in its town centre, grand in its view of hills and moors. Contemporary architecture has come here, too, but the history of cotton is still writ large through the place; and it should never be forgotten that in the workless days of the Thirties, when the mills were silent and the chimneys cold, Rochdale found work for its unemployed in helping to rebuild the town centre. Today it makes a large number of Pakistanis feel welcome. This is Gracie Fields's town, and her voice and humour symbolised a generation and its attitude as vividly as a Lowry painting. There's the *Rochdale Observer*, too, the newspaper that trained A. P. Wadsworth. And this is the town where the Co-operative movement was born in 1844, so Gracie knew what she was singing about when she sang of the "Co-op shop". The movement grew from one of the cotton industry's many regular depressions. A group of workmen, selling on ready money terms, opened a little shop and divided the profits among their customers. Rochdale feels less like a Manchester town than Bury does now, but it cannot wholly escape the magnet drawing it into the conurbation.

Apart from Salford, its unwilling Siamese twin, Manchester's most closely associated near-neighbour is the Cheshire town of Stockport, yet another town which has put off the armour of cotton and taken upon itself a multiplicity of industry. Its modern shopping centre has drawn people away from the parking nightmare of Manchester; the high flats have gone up on the hillside; the new roads and estates are built or are in the process of building. The railway viaduct is still there, of course, and Mersey Square, a motorist's Hampton Court Maze even in its supposedly simplified shape. Local loyalty, dour courage, municipal pride, Stockport has all these. There's 'nothing fancy' about Stockport, nor ever will be, I suspect, but it has lived through good times and bad, it has had a history of militancy in industrial disputes, and it will not easily surrender the ground it has gained. It shares with Manchester the attractive and fashionable residential suburbs of Bramhall, Hazel Grove and Heaton Mersey. Wilmslow is within easy reach.

It cannot be stressed often enough that the changes at present being wrought in Lancashire are as dramatic and far-reaching as those which transformed it 170 years ago. The second industrial revolution, the age of the computer and electronics, is in full transition, sweeping away not merely the perpetuated grimy and grim industrial image of Lancashire but changing the physical face of the county. What will come of it all only the future will show: no prophet could be sure enough to forecast whether the boom will last, whether the isolated pockets of unemployment are a portent or a freak, whether all this bulldozing and building will really produce a region to which the adjective grey will be as inappropriate as it is already unflattering. What, for instance, will be the impact on the Greater Manchester area of the vast new town planned further north in Lancashire, in the area of Chorley, Preston and Leyland, a town as yet unnamed, although Redrose, Ribbleton and Ribblesdale have been variously suggested?

The town, the largest concept of its kind yet envisaged for Britain, will be of 35,225 acres, with the Ribble Valley as its 'lung', safely preserved in all its natural beauty and historic interest. The population is estimated at 430,000, including a township of 60,000 to the north-east of the M6, by the end of this century. The Ministry which approved the scheme, after a lengthy public inquiry, says that its purpose is "to create a strong new centre of growth for Lancashire and to provide housing and employment for people now living in the appallingly congested, or decaying, areas of the North-west". Some other Lancashire towns, such as Blackburn and Burnley, are not so sure about this. Their fear, perfectly understandable, is that north-east Lancashire will be neglected by industry and government in favour of the new town development. Nor are the towns in south-east Lancashire all that happy. Bolton, for example, has expressed grave doubts, while pointing out also that the building of the town will lead to an urban sprawl from Wilmslow in the south through Manchester and Bolton to north of Preston—"like a little Los Angeles". The new town, Bolton's borough planner thinks,

> cannot do anything else but result in a reduction in capital for urban renewal available to places like Bolton. Bolton is already under some handicap in attracting industry by virtue of the development area status given to Merseyside and the intermediate status given to the Blackburn-Burnley-Colne area. Now we have this new town on our

doorstep. Although the Government says it will not have any special privileges regarding the location of industry I am utterly convinced that the Minister will persuade industrialists to go there to make the new town "tick" rather than go to Bolton.

The attitude of the Heath Government is crucial not only for Manchester but for the whole of Lancashire. (Although it comes outside the scope of this book, Liverpool and its environs present very special problems of industrial renewal and revival.) In an earlier chapter I used the phrase 'the idea of a city'. That is part of the wider concept 'the idea of a region'; and Manchester is a focal-point—one hesitates to say the capital—of a region much preoccupied with the idea of regionalism. It is a difficult philosophy to define, this regionalism, which is the fashionable word evolved to evade the supposedly pejorative implications of provincialism, a manifestation of the inferiority complex that often takes expression in an outward aggressiveness of local pride.

It is the worst mistake, the cardinal sin of parochialism, to assert that just because something is 'Northern' it therefore has some special quality which compensates for any deficiencies. If the North, and especially Manchester, wants to reclaim its place in the vanguard of national life it must take as its motto 'Only the best is good enough for us'. But the best won't be best simply because it originates in or is adopted by Manchester and the North. If one seeks a symbol of what I mean one can take nothing better than the career of the late beloved Kathleen Ferrier. From the sturdy bedrock of Blackburn came the great glory of that unique voice which had in it all the wonderful human qualities which we like to think of as typically Lancashire—warmth, understanding, humour and generosity. She rose like a comet from the world of competitive festivals. In a sense she was the astonishing—and very rare—apotheosis of amateur music-making. But all this would not have been enough. It was her seeking after perfection, the universal polish that she put on her art, that made her into an international artist and reflected glory on the county she loved and never deserted. Only the best was good enough for her: to sing Mahler under Bruno Walter, to sing Gluck at Covent Garden with Barbirolli, and to bring to Handel or Bach or Elgar at Belle Vue and Huddersfield all the artistry that was humanly possible.

It is folly for Mancunian Lord Mayors to cry "Woe, we are

neglected", if Manchester does nothing positive to ensure that
such neglect becomes unthinkable. Even so, the North does not
want to be patronised, to be given 'special' treatment. It merely
wants equal treatment. It is true that it should not be necessary
for a journalist or an actor or a singer or a lawyer or an engineer
or a doctor always to have to go to London to find the best outlet
for his particular talents, but equally it will continue to be necessary unless Manchester offers as fine a quality of life. It is folly to
ignore realities and to delude oneself into thinking that government from the centre, i.e. London, is going to stop and that
decentralisation on a huge scale will take place and give the
regions a status they have not had since the Wars of the Roses.
But the B.B.C. carried this view a bit too far when they practically
dismantled their regional set-ups and decided to encourage local
radio. The wise person says that when he switches on his television
set or radio he doesn't care where what he sees or hears is coming
from as long as it is worth seeing and hearing. But local radio on
the low budget assigned to it is bound to be parochial and paltry.

The great men of Manchester—whether they were born
Northerners or not—are those who have had a vision of 'the best'
and have worked to achieve it unheedful of the narrow limits of
local, or regional, pride. Manchester recognises this, as can be seen
from a glance through its roll of freemen. This, the city's highest
honour, has been sparingly given—only sixty-seven men and
women have been admitted to the roll in eighty-two years since
1888. It is instructive to read their names. If one excludes the war
heroes and war leaders—Churchill, Lloyd George, Haig, Mont-
gomery, Smuts etc.—one is still left with a remarkable gallery.
"Let us now praise famous men" because their example really is
what can make Manchester great again: Oliver and Abel Heywood, businessmen, sociologists and municipal politicians,
representative of the founders of Manchester's wealth and
outlook; Adolphus Ward, the man who more than any other
piloted Owens College to full university status; Enriqueta
Rylands, benefactress; Dr. Robert Christie and Sir Edward Holt,
whose names live on in the Christie Hospital and Holt Radium
Institute, one of the leading cancer establishments of the world;
William Houldsworth and Edward Donner, outstanding industrialists and benefactors of the city in dozens of ways; C. P.
Scott, who spread the city's name to the far ends of the world as

an upholder of the highest journalistic ideals and values; William Turner Jackson, who had the vision of Wythenshawe; Mary Kingsmill Jones and Wright Robinson, representative of the strongest and best tradition of government from the town hall; Lord and Lady Simon of Wythenshawe, separately for services which have been sufficiently outlined in this book; John Barbirolli, for giving Manchester's musical reputation added lustre and perhaps as amends for the absence of Charles Hallé's name from the roll; Matt Busby, for the kind of sportsmanship that transcends sport; John Stopford, vice-chancellor extraordinary. Common to them all was the belief that Manchester was a worthwhile idea in their field of activity. They were and are soldiers in the continuing battle against the philistines, whether ministerial, aldermanic or public.

TWELVE

STRICTLY PERSONAL

My principal qualification for writing this book is that, unlike many other people who have written about Manchester, I was born there and have worked there for thirty years. I love the place. It often annoys, infuriates and depresses me. I can see its faults, its limitations, its missed opportunities, its smugness, also its greatness of heart, its friendliness, its level-headedness, its common sense. Sometimes I think that the test of the true Mancunian is if he is held in thrall by the sight of the trees in Platt Fields on a foggy winter day. To me it is a beautiful, romantic, evocative sight, like my own favourite Manchester building (apart from the Town Hall), Lombard House, on the corner of Brown Street and Chancery Lane, where in imagination I can picture pre-Raphaelite Victorian damsels dressed like medieval princesses, standing on the pretty balconies and being serenaded by Ford Madox Brown—unlikely prospect, but a fair fancy.

I was born in Whalley Range, which is really Chorlton-cum-Hardy, not all that far from Old Trafford cricket ground. I cannot pretend that I was born within the sound of ball on bat—it was February, anyway—but on a still day in the summer when the traffic was quiet I imagine I could, while in my pram, have heard one of George Duckworth's "Owzats". My family had lived in Manchester for several generations, although both the Kennedys and the Sinclairs (my mother's family) came originally from Scotland. The cotton manufacturer James Kennedy, who has already been mentioned, was my great-great-grandfather, and if, as I believe, Kennedy Street was named in his honour, I feel I have the proprietorial right to walk along it with bayonet fixed and drums beating. My Kennedy great-aunt Amy married into the Worthington family, which is perhaps why I feel indulgent towards the Albert Memorial. But I am a rather unmancunian Mancunian. I went to school in the South of England, did not attend the university, have never lived in Didsbury, have never worked for the *Guardian*, and am not a Liberal.

My grandmother, a woman of remarkable character with the typical Lancashire combination of generosity and thrift, lived in Eccles. It was there that I spent many childhood days. It was a quieter suburb then, still basking, despite the Depression, in the afterglow of the prosperity that had given the Eccles Old Road the title of 'Millionaires' Row'. Although Salford and its slums, its Sally Hardcastles and Hanky Park, were only a mile or so up the road, Eccles was genteel and dowdily rich. Traffic was light and the road in which my grandmother lived was quiet and ended in green fields where today a housing estate stands. I remember the sunshine coming through the big bay window of her front room as I waited for the ice-cream man on his bicycle to ring his bell. There was a pleasant garden and lawn where I would play, and I remember the pungent smell of soot on the back wall and on the trees. When I climbed a tree I knew I should get into trouble because not only my hands, arms and legs but all my clothes would be black. My companion, a year or two older, was the grandson of the founders of Wiles's toy shop in Market Street. (He was killed in the war.) It was the thrill of the year to be taken there, for the most exotic and delightful toys were available.

When I was 2 or 3 my parents went to live in North Wales. Like many ex-officers from the 1914–18 war my father did not find it easy to settle to civilian life, and he was one of many who decided that poultry-farming was a good idea. So off to Towyn he went to keep hens, and when that failed he took to being landlord of a pub. North Wales has traditionally been part of the Mancunian's background. In those days and earlier it was the most favoured place for a holiday. Half Manchester moved in August to Deganwy, Rhyl, Conway, Rhos-on-sea and Anglesey.

My childhood seaside holidays were at Abergele which is the most un-seaside resort I know, because, for some reason I cannot define, it doesn't feel like the seaside; there is no sense, as there is in Cornwall or on the East Coast or even at Blackpool, of the omnipresence of the sea. There were pierrots on the beach, and those splendid old-fashioned machines in which W. G. Grace batted eternally against a moustached bowler if you put a penny in and wiggled the handles. Mancunians today retire to North Wales and end their days like Bertrand Russell in Colwyn Bay crematorium. I was quite happy at Abergele, but I dislike the North Wales coast intensely, and am glad that I experienced it early in my life: I shall not need to bother with it later.

It was there that I first became conscious of the existence of Manchester. One of the events of the day was the arrival and departure of 'the club train', in which many businessmen travelled daily to Manchester from Llandudno and other places. Occasionally my Worthington godfather would visit us, bringing with him an aura of Mancunian business. Everyone, it seemed to me, went to Manchester 'on business' or to see a specialist. It must, I thought, be a very important and serious place where everyone *worked*. London was a place where people went to enjoy themselves and Chester was where the shops were, but Manchester meant work.

When I went there as a boy to stay with my grandmother I liked to ride in the tram that rattled its way from Exchange through Salford to Eccles. At the front it had an advertisement for the Ship Canal, shown as a waterway of gorgeous royal blue. (For exaggeration of the truth I did not meet its equal until the Mancunian Way, which runs 'on stilts' across the city, was called 'the highway in the sky'.) The tram company's admonition to us was placed just above this advertisement, so that it read: "Do not spit in this car. Use the Ship Canal." My grandmother was not only a generous woman, she was wise. She treated me each year to the pantomime at the Palace Theatre, but did not go herself. I soon decided that one pantomime was very much like another, but at least I saw that great and forgotten comedian Jack Edge as an incomparable Idle Jack.

At $15\frac{1}{2}$ I left school, determined, before I had to join the war-time Services, to begin the career on which I had long set my heart, journalism. The first day I started work I walked into the big building in Manchester where in those days four morning newspapers and an evening were produced daily; and the smell of it all, a strange mixture of paper and machines and ink and chemicals, captivated me and still does.

The chief sub-editor under whom I first worked was a genial

yet ferocious Cockney. He never suffered fools at all, let alone gladly, and his powers of invective were colourful and strong. But if he thought you were trying, he was the best and most helpful of teachers, trenchant but sound, for as a newspaper 'technician' he had few equals. Some of his staff thought him uncouth, and I suppose he was, but he had an endearing softer side when he would quote poetry by the canto, and he enjoyed the mental exercise of devising his own verses in difficult forms and metres such as the sestina.

I am not the only journalist of my generation who is profoundly grateful to have come under his influence at a formative time. Once when I had my coat on ready to go home at about 11 p.m. he called out, "Come 'ere, yer young bugger. Where do you tell your mother you've been all evening?"

"I tell her I've been here."

"Do yer, by God! Well, you shouldn't, you should tell 'er you've been playing the piano in a brothel, it's more respectable than newspapers."

The editor of *The Daily Telegraph* in Manchester at that date was Oscar Pulvermacher, who had been a protégé of Northcliffe and held high office in Fleet Street during the days of the circulation wars. Legend said that he had been a master of in-fighting, and I have no doubt he was. He was cultured, distinguished, aloof and gave the impression of being a cold fish, though this was probably untrue if you knew him well. I should never have cared to have him as an enemy.

He gave me my first example of the unsentimental factual realism which characterises journalists and makes them the best company in the world. News seeped through from Finland in about 1942 that Sibelius was ill and likely to die. The chief subeditor, knowing I liked music, suggested I should try my hand at writing an obituary as an exercise. When I had recounted the facts of the composer's career the idealism of 16 got the better of me and I embarked on a purple passage about Sibelius's long silence since 1927. "Was it because of disillusion with the state of the world?" I asked. "Was he so dismayed by mankind's stupidity that he renounced it and determined to add no more of his wonderful music to its heritage? Is that why the eighth symphony has been denied us?" Or something awful to that effect. It was shown to Pulvermacher, who, in his bold and masterful handwriting, scrawled against my high-flown peroration the pungent comment: "No. Whisky."

Luckily I was on a naval course near Manchester in 1943 when John Barbirolli came to revive the Hallé after the B.B.C. players had left it. My friends and I were regular Hallé attenders, hearing it in the Opera House or in the suburban cinemas to which the bombing of the Free Trade Hall had condemned it. When this exuberant little man arrived from America we were amazed by the difference in the playing and excited by the electric atmosphere at the concerts. He managed to make you feel that each concert was the most important thing in life at that moment. No one who did not experience those early days can have any idea of the impact Barbirolli made nor fully understand why Manchester took him to its heart and kept him there and would not let him go.

Since then I have written music criticism in Manchester for over twenty years. I have heard hundreds of Barbirolli concerts, and Sir John himself was an old and beloved friend, charitably forgiving the follies of criticism because we shared a passion for music and for talking about it. He wore himself out in the service of music and the Hallé, never sparing himself physically or mentally, working fantastic hours, travelling, studying, rarely eating—or so it seemed.

To hear him talking about the great musicians with whom he had worked—and some of the not-so-great—was a constant source of pleasure, for his conversation was not only witty and wide-ranging but factually informative and detailed. He was one of the last of the great romantic conductors, possessed like Mahler by a daemon, able to charm and enchant the public like one of the old actor-managers and able, behind the scenes, to be as shrewd and keen as an economist, an artist who projected music in his own image and whose artistry, even when one disagreed with its application, always had integrity, intelligence and vitality.

When he became a Freeman of Manchester he described himself as an Italian-French-Cockney-Mancunian. It was this cosmopolitan background that gave John not only his superb artistic temperament but his rich humanity. He enjoyed working in Manchester, finding its rather serious air a suitable background for the musical adventures on which he and his audiences embarked. From the moment he arrived, he appreciated the candour of Lancashire folk. His favourite story of the 1943 days was of the young soldier who went to him at the interval for his autograph. J.B. signed and casually asked: "Are you enjoying the concert?" "Oh yes, Mr. Barbirolli, it's wonderful—*so far*!"

The wonders he performed in Manchester are well known; but whether Manchester ever did quite enough for him is debatable. His twenty-seven years with the Hallé can only be judged properly within the context of each decade. He was a pioneer at a time when the very idea of subsidising music was new and startling to the city council and he did his hardest work at a time of national austerity. 'What might have been' is always an unprofitable theme; Manchester should be thankful for what was. His friends mourn a lovable and magnetic man. Music mourns one of its greatest and most devoted servants.

Music and journalism have given me my most valued friendships. Although Neville Cardus has never lived or worked in Manchester during my professional life, we have been firm friends for many years and have kept open many a restaurant both in London and Manchester while we have talked music, cricket and journalism long after the doors should have been closed. Neville is the greatest talker I have known, and—which is rarer these days—one of the best correspondents. His letters convey his full flavour, as any reader of his books may imagine. But his conversation is like a cadenza played by Heifetz, and sometimes as unbelievable! Yet only a boring sobersides would chide Neville that some of his tales about the Lancashire cricketers of the 1920s are not factually true. What matters is that they are true to the characters of the men themselves. And if some of them have an immortality that their playing career would not have earned them, they owe that to Neville's pen and tongue.

At over 80 his figure is boylike, his step youthful, his mind razor-sharp. He's a wonderful human being, which is better than being a great man. And despite his love of London and his temptation to belong to other nations he remains at heart a Manchester man. We spent a summer day at Lord's which will stay in my memory as symbolic of Neville. The cricket was good but desultory, the crowd was small. We sat in one of the stands and talked of Elgar, Sammy Langford, Scott, Trumper and Emmott Robinson, while the Middlesex batsmen came and went just often enough to provide semi-colons for our converse. He has much in common with Barbirolli. Both must have looked at their younger selves in detached wonder as they contemplated the humble beginnings from which they sprang, and against which they did not have in any way the fashionable grudge, and marvelled at the eminence which was theirs through their own efforts and hard work. They personify the saying that you can't keep a good man down. Genius will out, whether it starts in Summer Place, Rusholme, or above a baker's shop in Holborn. Neville, like John, has the greatest gift the gods can bestow, apart from good health—a ripe sense of humour. One evening I called on John in his Salford house. "I've been writing hundreds of letters," he greeted me. "I've had to do this three times lately— first my twenty-five years with the Hallé, then the Companion of Honour, and now my 70th birthday. I said to the family, 'There's only one more lot to come now and those are the *condolences* and they're *your* job'." It was typical of his earthy attitude.

Mid-twentieth century Manchester has not been short of its giants, in achievement if not in physical stature. I am sure that the Mancunian of 2050 will look back with awe on the period in the city when it was peopled by men like Stopford, Barbirolli, Busby, Mansfield Cooper, Simon, Jefferson and Lowry; by Statham and Charlton; by Ollerenshaw, Pariser, Frederic Cox and A. P. Wadsworth. Philip Godlee, the man who brought Barbirolli to Manchester—Sir John called it "an act of Godlee"—a cavalier of business and the arts, tall, handsome, stricken by his war wounds but indomitable in spirit.

You had to get up early in the morning to catch Godlee out. He was a swashbuckler, in complete contrast to his successor as Hallé chairman. Leonard Behrens is the archetypal committee man, as a list of his achievements shows: Liberal Party president, Chamber of Commerce, University Convocation, College of Music Council, president of the Reform Club, vice-president of the United Nations Association—everything you can think of except captain of a golf club. He is the epitome of Mancunian liberalism in the arts, business, politics and social life with all its virtues, fads and failings. Leonard, like Cardus, has a sense of humour and this has prevented the atmosphere of his home from taking on the rather circumscribed and pompous elements which have been known to prevail elsewhere in Didsbury.

As the son of Gustav Behrens, he was brought up in the world of music, politics and the university. At Holly Royde, their family home which is now so appropriately and appreciatively used by the extra-mural department of the university, Leonard grew up accustomed to visitors like Joachim and Grieg, Brodsky and Richter, C. P. Scott and Samuel Alexander. It would be hard to discover a major Manchester organisation with which he has not at some time been associated—always excepting the sporting ones. Politics are his passion, but he failed to win the by-elections he contested. He has the gift of remaining on good terms with his opponents, and he and his wife Bebie have continued the honoured Didsbury tradition of gathering under their roof people whom they think ought to know one another or would like one another—a new professor, a gifted doctor or scientist, a new editor, a new member of the art gallery staff, an industrialist, all are invited to 'Netherby'. To call him a Manchester Man par excellence is the compliment Leonard Behrens would value highest.

Nor has the Manchester journalism of the past thirty years lacked its remarkable figures. As time recedes certain reputations emerge as outstanding. It seems to this non-*Guardian* writer that A. P. Wadsworth may be acclaimed by history as the greatest of *Guardian* editors; he was the last of its Manchester-based editors, and he imparted to the paper the lightness of touch, the pervading humour, the delicate mockery and even self-mockery, that give it a unique voice in the British Press. When space was rationed he gave Alistair Cooke plenty of space to indict McCarthyism. Nor was he deterred by charges of amateurishness which hardy professionals levelled at the paper: he knew his readers, and he embarked on the difficult task of transforming the Scott-Crozier *Guardian* of the pre-1939 epoch into the sort of paper that could survive, albeit precariously, in the economic climate of post-1945 publishing. He died before his work was done.

Many of those who achieve fame in Fleet Street—Arthur Christiansen, Harold Evans, Vincent Mulchrone, Malcolm Muggeridge—pass briefly through Manchester on their way. But they are not my concern here, for they hardly count as Manchester journalists in the full sense. Some depart and then return, like Brian Redhead, the ebullient editor-in-chief of the *Manchester Evening News*, who, building on the solid circulation amassed by the down-to-earth news sense of his predecessor, Tom Henry, has turned an evening paper into what the *Guardian* might still be if it had not transplanted its heart to London.

Guardian *sanctum*, C. P. Scott's *office*

Portland Street *palace*, Watts' *warehouse*

Brian is a North-Easterner, a Geordie, something that his speech betrays by its characteristic long vowels. "Halloooo, Michael Kennedeeee," he greets me; and that will be the prelude to a torrent of words. You have to be quick to get a word in with Brian, edgeways or any other way, but he is always fun and a provoker of provocative conversation. The speech he made at the dinner given by the Manchester Press to honour Neville Cardus's knighthood was described by the guest of honour as "like a Rossini overture"—a rare accolade from one prolific talker to another.

I have already described the blow to Manchester journalism dealt by the Munich air disaster. Sudden death has, in fact, been cruel to the sports writers of Manchester in recent years. To lose Henry Rose, Archie Ledbrooke, H. D. Davies and Eric Thompson in one day was something that still tears at the heart. Denys Rowbotham, the *Guardian*'s chief cricket writer, died young when at the height of his powers; and in R. H. Williams of *The Daily Telegraph* Soccer lost one of its wittiest, most knowledgeable and most percipient critics.

Bob Williams was my colleague and my friend, but it is not personal admiration alone that persuades me to rank him with Robertson-Glasgow as a writer on sports, for cricket and Rugby League were his field too. Big, friendly, uproarious in pub and club, good companion to colleagues of all ages and positions, sensitive lover of Elgar and Mahler and good singing, Bob was so alive that his death by drowning at the age of 40 while on holiday in Anglesey seemed, and still seems, like an offence against nature. You take such people for granted, except perhaps in wartime. When I look back to the seventeen years before 21st August 1969, I understand the real poignancy of Matthew Arnold's line "We still had Thyrsis then." By some deaths life is diminished for ever afterwards.

This book, I repeat, is a personal portrait of Manchester, and these names are my portrait gallery. There is one other which I have hesitated to include because by birth and conviction its bearer is a Salford citizen, and Salford is too independent a city to be used in these pages merely as an afterthought or appendage to its neighbour. Yet Harold Riley has put so much of Manchester into his work that it can surely claim a part of him.

In many private houses in the Manchester area your eye will

Barnes Wallis building, Institute of Science and Technology perhaps be caught by a painting or drawing of the urban scene or of a human face which arrests you by its strong yet poetic truth. This will be a Harold Riley. While still in his thirties Riley has achieved fame and selling-power in his own region which did not come till a later age to Lowry whom he so much admires. There could not have been Riley unless there had been Lowry first, but Riley has developed his own view of the Lancashire scene and its people which owes very little technically to Lowry.

Both share one quality that gives their work special merit. It is not propaganda, it is not politically motivated, it leaves the beholder to make the comments or to infer the message. Riley believes there is beauty in a Salford back street, in the lined careworn face of an old woman, in the houses and chimneys on the Oldham moors in the dawn. He does not romanticise or dramatise or bowdlerise what he sees, but he sees it with the eye of the true poet, and with the humanity and humour that so strongly characterise the man himself, lover of music, wine, football and his friends. He has steadfastly refused to desert the soil which has nurtured his art for the quick kill of a London reputation. Wisely, like Lowry, he paints and draws what he knows and sees, and if the connoisseurs wish to seek him out they must climb the steep stairs to the studio over the old coachman's cottage in Eccles. They climb them pretty often.

In many a Riley drawing I am reminded of the friendly, humorous, direct people whom one encounters daily in the city. I think that perhaps the main difference between life in London today and life in Manchester and other Northern cities is that people talk to each other a bit more and a bit longer: human contacts reach to a deeper level than just the give-and-take of a transaction over a counter. There is not the compulsion to be always 'in the fashion' or 'trendy'. The best and most revealing true Manchester anecdote I know is an experience which came the way of a newspaperman. There had been a particularly nasty murder in Ancoats or Beswick or somewhere of that kind. The husband had gone berserk and stabbed his wife and child and attacked other children. "Perhaps you'd better go out there and find out what sort of place it is and anything that's known about the family," the evening paper news editor said to a reporter who dutifully found the dingy terrace house where the murders had occurred. The door was opened by a grey, tired woman, probably the man's mother or mother-in-law. "Good afternoon," he said. "I'm from the . . ." She cut him short. "Nay, lad, not today, thank you. You see, we've 'ad a bit o' bother." You can find her type still, in the high flats and in the drawings of Harold Riley.

One can never be too grateful to artists like him who stimulate in us an appreciation of our surroundings which heightens our daily perceptions. How many Mancunians going about their bustling business stop and stare at one of the most attractive views to be found in any city—yes, in Manchester. Walk from King Street through St. Ann's Passage and look at the delightful vista of St. Ann's Church contrasted with the modern building on the left, separated by a paved walk. It is intimate yet formal, a sudden moment of privacy in the centre of a big city, ancient and modern all in one, framed by the archway of the arcade. I used to think that perhaps only an unrepentant Mancunian could take delight from this view until I discovered to my intense pleasure that my high opinion of it is shared by that architectural iconoclast Ian Nairn. I wish Lowry or Riley would draw it.

THIRTEEN

WHAT NEXT?

MANCHESTER has lost its way, they say. The red-blooded Athens of Commerce has come unstuck in the second half of the twentieth century. It has no purpose, no meaning. Liberalism and *laissez-faire* are dead; Britain does not need regional capitals, and, if it did, other cities have stolen the laurels from dreary old Manchester, still sighing for its Victorian heyday like a disconsolate dowager. That is the gist of the indictment. It is a superficial generalisation, but many would agree with it, shake their heads and sigh, and leave it at that.

Of course there is much cause for concern, and events in the past have sometimes shaken the confidence of the staunchest Mancunian. The way in which the corporation allowed several of the medieval halls in its care literally to fall to pieces showed a scant appreciation of the few remaining architectural treasures of pre-Georgian Manchester. Sir Nikolaus Pevsner has had harsh words to say about that, none of them unjustified.

Support for the arts has often been too little, too late and too grudgingly given when given: the city seems to have lost the knack of being an impresario; and when it puts on a show there is no panache and certainly no extravagance. The slowness in dealing with the traffic problem is another symptom of the arterio-sclerosis detected by some critics. Towns outside the city have built their new shopping centres, with parking space provided, while Manchester sends its shoppers on a tedious and often hopeless meter-crawl. High rents and rates and high land values have closed many a shop in Manchester or caused them to move to Wilmslow, Altrincham, Bramhall or Stockport. The public transport system needs radical reorganisation to serve the public in a wider variety of ways.

But look at all the building activity. How can this mean a city with nothing but a past? Look at the models of the New Manchester in the Town Hall. Look at the slum clearance and the new flats, with a realisable target of all unfit houses, 82,000 of them, demolished by the late 1970s. Look at the way black and white are living alongside each other with comparatively little friction, just as Jews and Turks and Germans and Greeks have lived alongside Mancunians for a century and a half. Look at the Shell plant at Carrington with millions of pounds poured into its development. Look at Trafford Park, alive with industry, and at I.C.I. Look at the development of new man-made fibres. Look at the names of the finance houses which have recently opened Manchester offices—Rothschild, Hill Samuel, Ansbacher, Bank of America, Société Générale. Would they be there if it was a dying city, a has-been awaiting the knock-out? Look at the municipally-owned airport at Ringway, developed with courage and foresight since the war into Britain's second busiest and most fog-free airport, with international links. (When the city council proposed to buy Ringway in 1934 the majority in favour was one vote.) Manchester has kept its trading lanes open by sea, air and road. Is there not enough evidence here of a city determined on greatness?

On the face of it the answer is yes. But can Manchester—can the whole area—keep the right people to make it great? Or must there be a continual brain drain to the South? Must industry lose its best research staff? Must the university lost its best professors? Must the Hallé conductor keep on training principals only to lose them to the London orchestras? The answer is no only if the quality of living in the Manchester area becomes second to none.

Nothing is more aggravating to the Northerner than the Southerner's idea that life in the North is second-class—unless it is the equally patronising propaganda of some Northern playwrights that everything in—well, Granadaland—is honest and hard-working and upright while everything in the South is phoney, shallow and devious, and probably gormless too. Generalisations such as these are, to those who know, ridiculous and insulting. Yet it is still too true that the man from Kent who is offered a post in the North, even though it carries more money, is more than likely to have the news received by his wife with despair and tears. What, move to the dirty North, with its smoke and rain and factories and black puddings and clogs and names like Boggart Hole Clough! Over my dead body. The image is outdated now, expressed like that, but it is still extant in places, which is why the 'Springclean' conducted by Sir William Mather and the Civic Trust is of continuing economic as well as psychological importance. But in washing our face we must beware that we do not scrub away all the wrinkles and lines that give us character. The North-west has character—it will not have it much longer if every town has the same pattern of shopping centre (no wonder they call them 'precincts'), if every block of flats looks like every other block of flats, if every motorway junction is just another stereotype. Take away the muck, by all means, but don't put only heartless hygiene in its place.

The future of Manchester must also be viewed as part of the future of the whole North-west region, of which it is the undisputed capital, for not even Liverpool would now challenge that valuation. National economic troubles have prevented as rapid a development of the region's industry as the North West Regional Economic Planning Council must have expected and there are still problems of unemployment in the Merseyside area despite the vast amount of state finance poured into it. (Who in Whitehall dreamed up the dreary phrase 'grey area' for parts of the North?) There are grave doubts whether the policy of giving piecemeal aid to local 'grey' pockets instead of to the region as a whole, as the Hunt Committee advised, is sensible especially when applied to the textile area of north-east Lancashire. Better, said the critics of the Wilson government's policy, to spend the money on planned location of industry, better roads and better housing throughout the region. Now it's up to the Conservatives.

The textile industry's labour force has been reduced by about 12,000 workers a year since 1950. Coalmining has had a comparable decline. These two factors govern the economic policy of the whole area. Textiles, in a state of flux for over a century one way and another, are in the midst of a further 'rationalisation', as the vogue-word euphemistically has it. The giants—Courtaulds, Viyella, I.C.I.—are battling for mergers while government committees inquire into the state of the industry. No other industry can have been inquired into more often and with less result.

While the 'big boys' of cotton manoeuvre into position and

while Whitehall talks, the smaller firms, fearing savage overseas competition from the end of the quota system and the substitution of too low a tariff on textile imports, await the future with trepidation. Forty per cent of the present industry of 100,000 workers is employed by about 370 smaller firms. Forecasts are that by 1975 these figures will be reduced to 55,000 and 135 respectively. In this sector the outlook is as uncertain as it has always been; it is at the crossroads.

Manchester, too, is at the crossroads, at a point of transition, at as significant a juncture in its affairs and history as it was in 1810. What could the city look like in 2000 if some of the plans nurtured by J. S. Millar, Manchester's planning officer, mature? First one might ask why the rebuilding of Manchester's centre has lagged, and the short answer is that the city was not bombed badly enough and that priority was given to housing. Gradually a comprehensive plan has taken over from the piecemeal development that led to the horrors of the Piccadilly site. Inter-connected open spaces in the King Street area, with St. Ann's Square traffic-free, are one possibility. The 30-acre site bounded by Market Street, Corporation Street and Withy Grove, at present a shabby district, is due for large-scale commercial development with large stores, small shops, banks, pubs, showrooms, an hotel and ample parking space. Market Street would become 'a landscaped pedestrian way', the backbone of a system of malls and arcades.

To make way for this gleaming paradise we shall have to lose some attractive little courts, some narrow twisting streets, the open-air bookstalls where you can still pick up a treasure for a few pence, and some historic and charming old pubs. But it has all happened before. Manchester's 'Second Town Plan' of 1821 was founded on the widening of Market Street, as a ballad-singer of the day—Ben Oldfield—duly recorded:

> Our Market Street was so narrow
> There was hardly room to wheel a barrow
> But now 'tis made so large and wide, sirs,
> Six carriages may go side by side, sirs,
> Sing heigh, sing ho, sing hey down gaily
> Manchester's improving daily.

There are plans to develop the area round the cathedral and Chetham's Hospital, involving demolition of the Corn Exchange (no loss), so that what was a focal-point of city life centuries ago regains its status. More new property will be built in the Old Shambles area, but the half-timbered Old Wellington Inn and Sinclair's Restaurant will be preserved and lifted by 6 feet to give them new foundations. A riverside walk is planned for a cleaned and beautiful Irwell, and if coarse fish ever return no one will be more delighted than the Dean, who still holds the fishing rights.

There will be more new buildings in Crown Square, near the Law Courts, opening up new views of John Rylands Library and stretching across to Albert Square, with the prospect of putting the Town Hall into even nobler perspective. There is good cause for optimism that the buildings to be erected will be architecturally impressive.

The planning officer can claim with accuracy that he has achieved co-operation and compromise between developers and planners by pointing to the splendid and unusual Gateway House, on the approach to Piccadilly Station, where the Regional Hospital Board is housed. This building is curved in a long 'S'. It cost more this way, but it was done because it will fit better with a new road crossing eventually to be built near the station.

Another plan is for 340 expensive residential flats in the Byrom Street-St. John Street area off Deansgate, a district that could become Manchester's Mayfair. This would be a first move in the campaign to persuade Manchester's businessmen to live in the city again.

All these plans, however, are dwarfed by the biggest Manchester plan of all which, when completed, may give the city the *raison d'être* it is seeking—as the greatest single higher educational centre in Europe, if not the world. On a 283-acre site a mile and a quarter long and 590 yards wide is being built a space-age campus which will unite in one town-within-a-town the university, the Institute of Science and Technology (a university in itself, presided over by Lord Bowden), John Dalton College of Technology, the Northern College of Music, the Regional College of Art, colleges of commerce, teacher training and medicine—45,000 students and staff, it is estimated, by the 1980s. A rebuilt Royal Infirmary will be part of the precinct, so will the National Computer Centre, a swimming-pool and ice rink, and an ecumenical centre. The cost will be not far short of £100 million.

This vast centre has Oxford Road like a spine down its centre and is bounded by Upper Brook Street and Princess Street to the east and Cambridge Street and Lloyd Street to the west, with an extension to London Road and Whitworth Street to take in some of the existing buildings of the Institute of Science and Technology. The site is crossed by the Mancunian Way 20 feet above ground level. Already the conception is taking shape, and in the seedy All Saints area the bulldozers have been busy: 700 homes, one hundred shops, thirty pubs and seven banks have disappeared.

Hugh Wilson and Lewis Womersley are the architects of this scheme, and in their 1967 final report they frankly acknowledged that the "significant fusion of town and gown" on a site so close to the city centre was the greatest danger of the project. "Because of the inevitable pressures on space and concern with day to day problems of implementation the big chance could be missed. . . . . The Precinct could become either a meeting ground for town and gown or a private intellectual enclave" (these, I am sure, are the words of Maurice Pariser). "If the latter should happen, it would be a tragedy for the city, the University and the Institute. We see this as a fundamental problem and have tried to keep in mind the need to achieve a degree of city renewal in its widest terms. . . . Every opportunity should be taken to achieve integration in deeds as well as in words." In other words, Manchester people must be encouraged to use the facilities of the university city. The architects have provided easy pedestrian access, the whole area being linked by footpaths, first-floor bridges and ramps. The fear must be that the whole thing could become too big and impersonal, a brain factory with no connections to the rest of the body. The phrase 'ripping the heart out of the city' is only acceptable as long as it applies to physical bricks and mortar; if it became spiritually true also, that would be disaster.

Planning is necessary and good, but only while it remembers one major factor: that cities are not inhabited by well-oiled, smooth-running machines but by people, stubborn, self-centred, irrational, unpredictable, independent people. The danger of planning when it forgets this simple fact has been demonstrated by the Wythenshawe experiment and even more drastically by Langley, Manchester's overspill estate at Middleton where vandalism and discontent have been rife for years and where the inhabitants complain that they belong to nobody, that the estate is heartless, that they miss the friendly neighbourliness of the old terraces and find blocks of flats anti-social. This is a major problem facing the new Manchester, for if nobody really takes an interest in the new estates, the city will lose its soul. If students and staff are at odds in the university, what price the new campus?

People are the most important part of a city, not its buildings. It is no coincidence that Manchester has a long tradition of social service, pioneered by men like Henry Gaddum and continued by the Council of Social Service which interests itself in the health and welfare of citizens in all walks of life. No welfare state can provide a substitute for the good Samaritan who, unpaid and from the kindness of his heart, cares for his fellow beings. When Will Fyffe sang "I belong to Glasgow" he was expressing everything good that flowed from the vitality of a great city notwithstanding the squalor. The single great aim of the planners and government of Manchester in the next twenty-five years must be to encourage people to say "I belong to Manchester." Then will follow the inevitable and right corollary, "Manchester belongs to me."

No doubt the pattern of the city's life will change beyond all recognition, for we cannot really tell what may happen over the next half century. Which Mancunian in 1780 could have foretold the city of 1830? The only symbol that can safely be laid against the future of Manchester is a question-mark, but it would be lily-livered to end so indecisively. Yet in 1970 can I honestly echo the ballad-singer of 1820 and say "Manchester's improving daily"? I will put it this way: despite the very real danger that the city will refuse to 'think big' enough to match the boldness of some of the schemes affecting its survival as a major force in national life, I cling stubbornly to the faith that what Manchester did yesterday it can do again, and better, tomorrow. And, as we say in Lancashire, "Ah'm not arguin'. Ah'm tellin' thee."

INDEX

Adamson, Daniel, 86
Agate, James, 100, 131, 140
Agricola, Julius, 17, 117
Albert Square, 26, 75, 83, 85, 109, 184
Alderley Edge, 84, 120, 152, 153
Alexander, Samuel, 93, 176
Altrincham, 19, 23, 84, 152, 153, 180
Ancoats, 23, 55, 57, 58, 61, 77, 93, 178
Ancoats Brotherhood, 106
Anti-Corn Law League, 73-4
Architecture, 77-85
Ardwick, 21, 47, 48, 54, 117, 156, 160
Arkwright, Sir Richard, 35, 91, 161
Armitage, Arthur, 136
Art Treasures Exhibition, 94-5, 96, 104, 117
Ashton-under-Lyne, 20, 21, 28, 62, 66, 71, 72, 153
Attlee, 1st Earl, 16
Aytoun Street, 78

Bamford, Samuel, 65, 69
Banking Development, 38, 45, 70
Barbirolli, Sir John, 92, 98-9, 109, 112, 113, 128, 157, 166, 168, 173-4, 175
Barlow, R. G., 13, 118, 122
Barry, Sir Charles, 25, 44, 104
Barton Aqueducts, 34, 87
Beecham, Sir Thomas, 25, 98, 107, 109, 112
Behrens, Gustav, 97, 175
—— Sir Leonard, 175-6
Belle Vue, 112, 166
Bernstein, Lord, 103
Best, George, 116, 117
Bexwicke, Richard, 29
Birkett, Lord, 148, 155
Blackburn, 31, 165, 166
Blackett, Lord, 137, 139
Blackley, 21
Blanketeers, March of, 63-4
Bolton, 19, 31, 58, 61, 62, 66, 82, 103, 106, 152, 154, 156, 165-6; and Maud Report, 159-62

Bowdon, 23, 84, 89, 97, 109, 121, 152, 153
Bramhall, 19, 117, 152, 164, 180
Brandt, C. F., 35, 39, 41
Brazennose Street, 26, 67, 83
Bridge Street, 55
Bridgewater, 3rd Duke of, 34
Bridgewater Canal, 34, 87
Bridgewater Street, 17
Bright, John, 27, 73, 79, 149, 164; and Manchester School, 74-5
Brindley, James, 34, 87
Brodsky, Adolph, 97, 106, 118, 176
Broughton, 54, 84
Bury, 19, 22, 31, 58, 66, 152, 156, 163-4
Busby, Sir Matt, 113-17, 168, 175
Buxton, 17, 47
Byrom, John, 27, 32, 34, 61

Campfield, 44
Canute, King, 20
Cardus, Sir Neville, 118-20, 138, 155-6, 174-5, 177
Carpenter, R. H., 25
Castlefield, 17, 34
Castle Irwell (racecourse), 18
Cateaton Street, 21, 32
Central Library, 25, 82, 85, 103, 106, 111
Central Station, 58
Chamber of Commerce, 45, 70, 88, 175
Champneys, Basil, 24, 84
Charles Edward Stuart, Prince, 27, 61-2, 95
Charlotte Street, 40, 42
Charlton, Bobby, 114, 115, 116, 175
Charters (for Manchester), 21, 58-60
Chat Moss, 17, 46
Cheadle, 19, 152
Cheshire, 17, 18, 19, 22, 101, 120-22, 123, 124, 141, 152, 153
Chester, 30, 40, 121, 161, 171

Chetham's Hospital School, 20, 22, 39, 110, 144-6, 183
Chopin, Frédéric, 25, 96
Chorlton-cum-Hardy, 156, 169
Chorlton-on-Medlock, 44, 48, 54, 57, 77
Churchill, Sir Winston, 16, 75, 79, 167
C.I.S. Building, 27, 85
City Art Gallery, 25, 42, 44, 90, 92, 103-4, 105, 107
Civil War, 61, 161
Clayton, 21, 113, 140
Cobden, Richard, 59, 78, 89, 93, 146;
and Corn Laws, 73-5
Cockerell, Charles, 79
College of Clergy, 22, 28, 30, 31
Collegiate Church, see Manchester Cathedral
Collyhurst, 21
Comedy Theatre, 26, 101
Conran, G. L., 90
Corn Exchange, 44, 183
Corn Laws, 27, 63, 65, 73-4, 77
Coronation Street, 111, 158
Corporation Street, 27, 183
Court Leet, 32, 34, 39, 59, 60
Cox, Frederic R., 175
Crompton, Samuel, 35, 62, 160-61
Cross Street, 26-7, 43
Cross Street Chapel, 33, 41
Crozier, W. P., 134, 137, 176
Crumpsall, 21, 30

Daily Telegraph, 172, 177
Dalton, John, 25, 27, 41, 53n., 57, 82, 97, 138
Davies, H. D., 115, 119, 177
Deansgate, 20, 21, 22, 24, 25, 26, 32, 34, 55, 58, 83, 84, 184
Defoe, Daniel, visits Manchester, 33
Denton, 58, 80, 138, 153
Depression of 1930s, 23, 105, 118, 164
De Quincey, Thomas, 41, 143
Derby, Earls of, 29, 61, 144; 7th Earl beheaded, 161-2
Derbyshire, 19, 22, 78, 122, 153
Dickens, Charles, 56, 57, 79

Dickinson, John, 62
Didsbury, 19, 21, 58, 84, 89, 103, 156, 170; its influence, 129-30
Disraeli, Benjamin, 57, 75
Doherty, John, 65, 72
Drinkwater, Peter, 51, 62-3
Duckworth, George, 118, 169

Eccles, 19, 46, 48, 51, 84, 87, 153, 170, 171, 178
Edward the Elder, 19
Edwards, Duncan, 114, 115
Elgar, Sir Edward, 79, 97, 112, 162, 166, 174, 177
Engels, Frederick, 27, 52, 54-5
Exchange Station, 22

Failsworth, 17
Fairbairn, Sir Thomas, 93
—— Sir William, 58, 140
Fallowfield, 84, 130, 136, 143, 146, 156
Faucher, Léon, 52-3
Fennel Street, 32, 77
Ferrier, Kathleen, 27, 166
Fields, Gracie, 52, 118, 160, 164
Fiennes, Celia, 33
Flowers, Sir Brian, 139
Fountain Street, 31, 38, 40, 95, 100
Fraser, Bishop, 93, 100
Free Trade, 13, 73-5
Free Trade Hall, 16, 26, 27, 73, 82, 96, 107, 111, 173; built, 74, 78-9
Friends' Meeting House, 44

Gaddum, Henry, 186
Gaiety Theatre, 26, 101, 102
Garnett, Jeremiah, 45
Gaskell, Elizabeth, 23, 41, 57, 95
—— Reverend William, 41
Gateway House, 184
Gentlemen's Concerts, 25, 95, 96, 101, 142; hall built, 38
George Street, 38
German colony, 18
Godlee, Philip, 98, 99, 175
Goodwin, Francis, 43-4, 81
Gorton, 21, 58, 63
Granada Television, 57, 103, 181

Grant, William and David, 56
Greater Manchester, 19, 121-2, 151-68
Greg, Robert, 57, 73
Grelley, Albert, 20
—— Robert, 20-21
—— Thomas, 21, 28
Guardian, The, 13, 27, 98, 100, 111, 129, 170, 176, 177; founded, 45; its influence, 130-35

Hale, 84, 152, 153
Haley, Sir William, 127
Hallé, Sir Charles, 25, 27, 79, 95-7, 99, 142, 168
Hallé Orchestra, 13, 43, 79, 91, 97-9, 107, 108, 109, 111, 112, 117, 125, 173
Hanging Ditch, 21, 27, 32, 44
Hanson, Thomas, 63
Hargreaves, James, 35, 161
Harris, Vincent, 85
Harrison, Thomas, 40, 43
Harty, Sir Hamilton, 98, 99
Heaton Norris, 21
Heaton Park, 44
Henry, T. E., 176
Henry Watson Music Library, 25
Henshaw's Institute, 44
Heron, Joseph, 59
Hetherington, Alastair, 134-5
Heyrick, Richard, 61
Heywood, Sir Benjamin, 41, 45, 80
Highs, Thomas, 35
Hornby, A. N., 13, 118
Horniman, Miss, 26, 101
Howitt, Leonard, 79
Hulme, 23, 24, 44, 54, 55, 57
Hulton, William, 68
Hunt, Henry, 23, 65; at Peterloo, 66-8
—— Holman, 92, 104
Huntington, John, 28
Hunt's Bank, 32, 33

Irk, River, 17, 30, 32, 55, 62, 141; grinding mill on, 20-21; its eels, 22
Irwell, River, 17, 20, 22, 30, 32, 33, 34, 46, 56, 87, 99, 156, 184

Jackson, W. T., 123, 125, 168
James of Rusholme, Lord, 143
Jefferson, Sir Geoffrey, 137, 141, 175
Jodrell Bank, 127
John Dalton Street, 81
John Rylands Library, 24, 84, 184
Joule, J. P., 138-9

Kay, Dr. James, 51-2, 55
—— John, 163
Kendal, Milne, 20, 24
Kennedy, James, 71, 169
Kersal, 32, 34, 113
King Street, 26, 34, 38, 45, 47, 59, 79, 81, 83, 85, 121, 179, 183
Knott Mill, 20, 24, 63
Knutsford, 17, 23, 120, 121, 153

Lake District, 18, 156; source of water, 147-9
Lancashire, 17, 19, 30, 57, 61, 86, 105, 106, 141, 150, 153, 155, 156, 162; county cricket, 117-20; proposed new town, 165-6
Lane, Richard, 44, 80
Langford, Samuel, 98, 131, 174
Langley, Ralph, 28-9
La Warr, Thomas, 28, 29, 144
Ledbrooke, Archie, 115, 177
Lees, Charles, 162
Leland, John, describes Manchester, 30-31
Leo, Hermann, 95-6
Liberalism, 13, 70, 75-6, 89, 130, 180
Library growth, 38, 39-40, 106
Library Theatre, 103
Literary and Philosophical Society, 38, 41, 92, 138
Liverpool, 18, 33, 35, 40, 46, 47, 56, 61, 70, 78, 107, 113, 121, 151, 156, 166, 182
Liverpool Road Station, 46
Lloyd George, David (1st Earl), 27, 79; and Scott, 75-6
Lombard House, 169
London Road, 17, 25, 49, 58, 84, 185
Long Millgate, 21, 29, 32, 55, 141
Longsight, 58, 112
Lovell, Sir Bernard, 127

Lowry, L. S., 105, 112, 157, 164, 175, 178, 179
Lutyens, Sir Edwin, 25, 85

Macalpine, J. B., 140
Macclesfield, 64, 71, 152, 153
Madox Brown, Ford, 81–2, 106, 169
Malibran, Maria, 27, 42
Mamucium, 17
Manchester Cathedral, 20, 22, 24, 27, 32, 50, 60, 75; proposed new site, 25; features of, 28–9
Manchester City F.C., 113, 117
Manchester Corporation, 60, 86, 99, 104, 108, 109
Manchester Evening News, 85, 127, 176
Manchester Grammar School, 38, 110, 141–4; founded, 29–30
Manchester Guardian, see Guardian, The
Manchester–Liverpool Railway, 42, 45–6
Manchester medical school, 140–41
Manchester School, 74–5
Manchester Ship Canal, 13, 18, 86–8, 127, 157, 171; first proposed, 70
Manchester United F.C., 13, 18, 23, 43, 113–17; Munich crash, 114–16
Manchester University, 93, 109–10, 136–9; development plan, 184–5
Mancunian Way, 24, 44, 171, 185
Mancunium, 17
Mansfield Cooper, Sir William, 137–8, 175
Market Street, 25, 26, 32, 43, 45, 56, 58, 62, 74, 170, 183
Marx, Karl, 27
Mason, P. G., 143, 144
Mather, Sir William, 182
Mather and Platt, 58
Maud Report, 151–4, 155, 156–7, 159, 163
Mechanics' Institution, 45
Medlock, River, 17, 55, 56
Mercer, Joe, 113, 117
Mersey, River, 17, 30, 33, 130
Methodism, 23, 53, 71
Midland Hotel, 25, 26, 82, 83, 95, 101, 102
Miller, Douglas, 143

Mobberley, 120, 121, 153, 155
Monkhouse, Allan, 100, 101, 131
Montague, C. E., 98, 100, 131, 132, 135
Mosley family, 31, 34, 60, 61
Mosley Street, 25, 31, 39, 40, 41, 42, 44, 47, 57, 78, 79, 95, 103
Motorways, 18
Mount Street, 26, 44, 67, 82, 100
Muggeridge, Malcolm, 133–4, 176
Munich air crash, 27, 114–16, 117, 177

Nadin, Joseph, 64, 68
New Bailey Prison, 60, 69
New Cross, 68, 80
Newman, Ernest, 98, 131
Newton Heath, 58, 113, 138
Northern College of Music, 110, 146, 184
Northern School of Music, 110

Octagon Theatre, 103, 159–60
Ogdon, John, 143
Oldham, Hugh, 29–30, 141
Oldham, 17, 19, 22, 58, 62, 66, 71, 152, 156, 160, 162–3, 178
Old Trafford, 23, 94, 113, 116, 148, 169; cricket at, 117–20
Old Wellington Inn, 32, 184
Ollerenshaw, Kathleen, 147, 175
Openshaw, 21, 140
Opera House, the, 24, 93, 102, 173
Opera house projects, 25, 107–8
Ordsall Hall, 158–9
Owen, Robert, 51
Owens, John, 93
Owens College, 93, 100, 139, 167
Oxford Road, 55, 80, 83, 93, 102, 184

Palace Theatre, 101, 102, 171
Pariser, Sir Maurice, 107–8, 175, 185
Parkin, Cecil, 23–4, 118–19
Parsonage, The, 20
Paton, J. L., 143
Peak District, 18, 122
Peel, Sir Robert, 74, 158, 163
Pendlebury, 83, 153
Pendleton, 54
Pennine Hills, 17, 18, 30, 150

Percival, Dr. Thomas, 38
Peterloo, 16, 26, 45, 64–70, 76, 78, 82
Peter Street, 26, 32, 55, 100, 101
Piccadilly, 25, 32, 34, 42, 49, 58, 78, 85, 107, 183
Piccadilly Plaza, 25, 42
Pilkington, Margaret, 105
Platt, Sir Harry, 137, 140, 141
—— Lord, 137, 141
Police Commissioners, 39, 51, 59–60
Population, 18, 20, 33, 34, 35, 43, 51, 58, 59
Portico Library, 25, 39–43, 57–8, 105
Portland Street, 25, 51, 67, 78, 84, 140
Potter, Thomas, 59
Prentice, Archibald, 69–70
Prestbury, 120
Preston, 18, 165
Prestwich, 17, 19, 44, 109, 153
Princess Street, 25, 35, 39, 42, 55, 81, 185
Princes Theatre, 101–2
Puccini, Giacomo, 26
Pulvermacher, Oscar, 172

Quay Street, 24, 33, 55, 93, 102, 103
Queen's Hotel, 78

Railways, 45–7, 58
Redcliffe-Maud, Lord, 151, 152, 155, 157, 159
Redhead, Brian, 176–7
Reform, Struggles for, 59–60, 63–70
Reform Club, 26, 83, 85, 175
Regional College of Art, 110, 184
Richter, Hans, 97, 98, 99, 118, 125, 176
Riley, Harold, 177–9
Ringway Airport, 18, 153, 181; memorial at, 85–6
Riots in Manchester, 35, 62–71
Roberts, Sir Leslie, 87
Rochdale, 19, 31, 58, 66, 152, 156, 163, 164
Roger of Poitou, 20
Roget, Peter Mark, 41
Rolls-Royce, 27, 140
Roman Occupation, 17, 19
Roscoe, Henry, 93, 139

Rosworm, John, 61
Rowbotham, Denys, 177
Rowley, Charles, 106
Royal Exchange, 26–7, 34, 43, 62, 63, 162
Royal Infirmary, 25, 41, 184; early origins, 34
Royal Manchester College of Music, 97, 103, 110, 118, 162, 175
Royal Manchester Institution, 44–5, 92, 103, 104
Rusholme, 102, 175
Rutherford, Lord, 27, 139
Rylands, Enriqueta, 84, 167

St. Ann's Church, 43, 179
St. Ann's Square, 21, 26, 34, 38, 43, 80, 183
St. Ann Street, 21, 26, 80
St. George's Church, Hulme, 44
St. John Street, 24, 47, 67, 184
St. Mary's Church, 20
St. Mary's Church ('Hidden Gem'), 83
St. Mary's Gate, 20
St. Peter's Church, 25, 42
St. Peter's Field, 23, 26, 63, 65; and Peterloo, 67–8, 74
St. Peter's Square, 25, 39
Saintsbury, George, 11, 68, 131
Sale, 19, 23, 30, 89, 152, 153
Salford, 17, 19–20, 21, 24, 30–31, 32, 34, 44, 45, 46, 47, 54, 56, 61, 69, 82, 83, 97, 100, 105, 106, 110, 152, 153, 160, 164, 170, 171, 175, 177, 178; and Maud Report, 156–9
Scott, C. P., 27, 92–3, 97, 100, 104, 130, 136, 137, 139, 142, 167–8, 174, 176; and Liberalism, 75–6; his editorship, 131–4
—— E. T., 134
—— Sir George Gilbert, 80, 83
—— Laurence, 134
SELNEC, 19, 152–3, 155, 163
Shankland, Graeme, 160
Shaw, George Bernard, 100–101, 106
Ship Canal, see Manchester Ship Canal
Shudehill, 32, 35, 62

Simon, Henry, 97, 125
Simon of Wythenshawe, Lady, 124, 128–9, 147, 168
—— Lord, 124, 125–8, 131, 168, 175
69 Company, 103
Smoke, 13, 34, 50, 52; abatement, 149–50
Southey, Robert, 48; description of town, 50
Spring, Howard, 67, 132
Spring Gardens, 31, 35, 38, 100
Stables Theatre, 103
Stanley, James, 29
Statham, J. B., 116, 119, 120, 175
Stephenson, George, 46
Stockport, 17, 19, 44, 46, 49, 58, 59, 61, 65, 68, 71, 152, 156, 164, 180
Stopford of Fallowfield, Lord, 127, 136–7, 138, 140, 141, 168, 175
Strangeways, 17, 51, 80
Stretford, 19, 23, 82, 117, 153, 156
Swift, Frank, 115, 117
Swinton, 19, 153

Tatton family, 123
Tatton Park, 121
Taylor, John Edward, 45; his son, 131, 132
Temple, William, 75
Textile trade, 30, 31–2, 35, 70, 160–61, 162, 182–3
Theatre Royal, 38, 43, 100
Thompson, Francis, 118
Tib, River, 42
Town Halls: first, 43–4, 59, 81; second (Waterhouse's), 26, 81–2, 85, 111, 169, 181, 184
Trades Union Congress, 27, 72
Trafford Park, 23, 30, 87, 140, 181
Tyldesley, Richard, 118, 155–6

Ullswater, 147–9, 155
University Institute of Science and Technology (UMIST), 110, 184
Urmston, 19, 153

Vickers, Harry, 146
Victoria, Queen, 35, 48, 60, 86–7

Victoria Bridge, 22
Victoria Park, 48, 58, 84, 97
Victoria Station, 46
Victoria University, see Manchester University
Victorian Gothic, 24, 80–84

Wadsworth, A. P., 134, 137, 164, 175, 176
Walker, F. W., 142
Walmsley, Robert, 66, 68, 69
Walters, Edward, 78–9, 136
Walton, Sir William, 162–3
Ward, Sir Adolphus, 93, 100, 131, 136, 167
Warrington, 35, 62, 152, 153, 156
Waterhouse, Alfred, 80–2, 85, 93, 142
Water supply, 31, 147–9
Watts' Warehouse, 78
Weizmann, Chaim, 139
Wellington, 1st Duke of, 42, 46
West, Thomas, 29
Westhoughton, 63, 153; and over-spill, 154–6
Whit Walks, 113
Whitworth, Sir Joseph, 58, 104, 136, 140
Whitworth Art Gallery, 83, 105
Whitworth Street, 81, 83, 84, 185
William Hulme Grammar School, 146
Williams, R. H., 177
Wilmslow, 84, 109, 120, 121, 153, 164, 165, 180
Wilson, Harold, 108, 182
—— Hugh, 185
Windmill Street, 26
Withington, 21, 84, 127, 130, 156
Withy Grove, 32, 34, 183
Womersley, Lewis, 185
Worsley, 34, 46, 80, 153
Worthington, Thomas, 80, 82–3
Wren, Sir Christopher, 44
Wythenshawe, Lord Simon of, see Simon of Wythenshawe, Lord
Wythenshawe, 123–5, 127, 185

Yorkshire, 17, 18, 23, 162